P9-BZT-750

DON'T BREAK THE BANK: COLLEGE EDITION

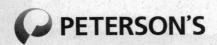

About Peterson's

Peterson's provides the accurate, dependable, high-quality education content and guidance you need to succeed. No matter where you are on your academic or professional path, you can rely on Peterson's print and digital publications for the most up-to-date education exploration data, expert test-prep tools, and top-notch career success resources—everything you need to achieve your goals.

For more information, contact Peterson's, 3 Columbia Circle, Suite 205, Albany, NY 12203-5158; 800-338-3282 Ext. 54229; or find us online at www.petersonsbooks.com.

ISBN-13: 978-0-7689-3765-7

First Edition

By producing this book on recycled paper (40% post-consumer waste), 40 trees were saved.

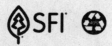

Sustainability—Its Importance to Peterson's

What does sustainability mean to Peterson's? As a leading publisher, we are aware that our business has a direct impact on vital resources—most especially the trees that are used to make our books. Peterson's is proud that its products are certified to the Sustainable Forestry Initiative (SFI) chain-of-custody standard and that all of its books are printed on paper that is 40 percent post-consumer waste using vegetable-based ink.

Being a part of the Sustainable Forestry Initiative (SFI) means that all of out vendors—from paper suppliers to printers—have undergone rigorous audits to demonstrate that they are maintaining a sustainable environment.

Peterson's continuously strives to find new ways to incorporate sustainability throughout all aspects of its business.

Dear Reader:

Many people have a love-hate relationship with money. They do not like dealing with it, worrying about it, and working at jobs they may not love in order to earn it. But they also realize that money is sort of a necessary evil. From a practical standpoint, we all know that it is impossible to survive without it.

Of course, money itself isn't necessarily bad. It's just that people often display bad behavior in order to get money and then may have bad habits related to spending it.

But if you educate yourself about the responsible ways to handle money, and exercise self-control when it comes to spending it, money can be a good thing. It is what you will use to support yourself and your family, to buy things you need (and, if budget allows, things you want), and also to pay for things like education, travel, family vacations, and other experiences you will enjoy.

Of course, first you have to learn important things about money—such as how to earn it, smart strategies for spending it wisely, and the best ways to invest it.

Learning about money is very important at this stage of your life because, most likely, you are starting to gain some financial independence and handle your own money as an adult. You have college tuition bills and other expenses, and you may have a job or two in order to pay your bills. It's important that you have the tools to help you understand how to handle money wisely so that you can pay your bills and manage your money—without getting into financial trouble.

This book will help you become financially savvy by explaining

- important aspects related to earning money
- tips for stretching it and sticking to a budget
- the pros and cons of credit
- advice for saving for your future

And much more!

We hope you will find this publication useful in helping you increase your financial know-how. Peterson's publishes a full line of books—financial aid, career preparation, test prep, and education exploration.

Other Peterson's books you may find helpful include the following:

- *Best Scholarships for the Best Students*
- *The "C" Students Guide to Scholarships*
- *How to Get Money for College*
- *Scholarships, Grants & Prizes*

Peterson's publications can be found at high school guidance offices, college libraries and career centers, and your local bookstore and library. Peterson's books are now also available as eBooks and online at www.petersonsbooks.com.

We welcome any comments or suggestions you may have about this publication. Your feedback will help us make educational and financial dreams possible for you—and others like you.

Sincerely,

Peterson's Editorial Staff

CHAPTER ONE: MONEY BASICS

BANKING

By this point in your life, it's likely that you already have a checking and/or savings account and probably have lots of experience with money and financial transactions—including shopping online and buying things at a store using methods other than cash. However, we're willing to guess that you haven't given much thought to what goes on behind the scenes and how the whole process actually works. And you may not know much about the banking system and what happens to allow you to use that debit card or write out that check.

In some ways, banking is much easier now than it was in the past. In many cases, you can handle a lot of your money-related tasks from home or wherever you happen to be, without ever going near an actual bank.

In other ways, though, the process is a lot more complicated, partly because you have so many more options. There are a lot of special types of savings and checking accounts—and many ways to access those accounts, including online, by phone or using a smartphone or other device.

We'll discuss some of the various systems involved with the banking process and delve into some specific banking-related topics, and we think you'll discover some interesting things you didn't know—and possibly learn a few tips that might make your financial life a bit easier.

THE FDIC IS YOUR FRIEND

The important thing to know about the FDIC is that it protects banking customers against loss should something strange or unexpected happen to a bank. Here's a brief explanation of the FDIC from their website at (http://www.fdic.gov) .

EXPERT ADVICE

When you are getting ready to head off to school, carefully consider bank options ahead of time. Most (if not all) colleges have a bank or ATM on campus. Plan ahead before school starts, and learn your options. Try to open an account with the bank or credit union on campus to avoid paying ATM fees if your hometown bank is not the same.

From American Consumer Credit Counseling

"The FDIC—that's short for Federal Deposit Insurance Corporation—is part of the U.S. government. Congress created the FDIC in 1933 after a terrible economic period called 'The Great Depression' when thousands of banks shut down and families and businesses all across America lost money they had deposited in those banks. The FDIC's primary job is to make sure that, if a bank closes, all of the bank's customers will get their deposits back—including any interest they've earned—up to the insurance limit under federal law. In the eighty years since the start of the FDIC, we have responded to about 3,000 bank failures, and we are proud to say that no depositor has lost a single penny of insured money."

SAVINGS ACCOUNTS

Traditionally, most people's first experience with the banking system was in the form of a savings account. In the past, when you opened a savings account, you would get a little book that looked similar to a passport where the tellers would write or type entries about your deposits, withdrawals, and other financial transactions.

These days, you access your account information online, and you will likely just receive an ATM card, which you will use to access your money and get account information.

2

You may have had a savings account since you were a kid—but if you opened the account before you were 18 years old, you probably had to have a joint account, where a parent or guardian also was listed on the account. Once you reach the age of a legal adult, you can open accounts on your own.

Today, you can often open several different types of accounts at once. It's common for people to open both a checking and savings account simultaneously. The checking account is generally used for daily banking like paying bills and buying groceries, whereas the savings account (as you can guess from the name) is used to accumulate a fund that might be used in case of an emergency or for some long-term goal, such as paying for college or buying a car.

A smart strategy is to "link" your accounts together—which is usually easy if they are all with the same bank. One advantage to doing this is the ability to set up automatic transfers. For example, if you want to put a certain amount of money in your savings every week (or every payday), you can set it up so that the bank automatically transfers that amount from your checking account into your savings account.

Another smart thing to do with linked accounts is set up overdraft protection. This means that if your checking account becomes overdrawn (or is at risk of being overdrawn), the bank will automatically take the money from your savings account in order to cover or prevent the overdraft. This can be very helpful, because it saves you from incurring overdraft fees—which can be very high—and also helps prevent your checks from being returned unpaid, or having pending charges refused, which can be very embarrassing.

When you make a deposit, those funds may not be available in your account right away. This is especially true if you are depositing a check or other non-cash currency. The bank may wait for that check to clear before crediting it to your account. Check your bank's website (or look for signs in your local branch) for their funds' availability policies.

Savings accounts allow you to earn interest on your money, although the rate of interest you will earn usually isn't very high.

UNDERSTANDING INTEREST

It's almost impossible to talk about banking without discussing interest, which is basically a fee paid for borrowing or using someone else's money. (Keep in mind, that "someone" may not refer to an actual person—it also can mean a bank, credit union, or other business or financial institution.)

You might say interest is a two-way street. It can go in either direction, depending on the type of transaction involved.

In the case of a savings account or other type of interest-earning account, the bank pays you interest, in return for letting them "hold" (and use) your money. On the other hand, if you are borrowing money in the form of a loan or mortgage, then you would be the one paying the bank interest.

Interest works on a percentage basis. So the amount of interest will depend on the amount of money you save or borrow. The current interest rate fluctuates according to the economy. A bank employee can give you information about the current interest rate.

HOW YOUR MONEY GROWS

While the interest rate for your savings account may not seem very high, you might be surprised at how quickly it can add up!

That's due in large part to the concept of "compound interest." That's a little complicated but here's the basic idea: when you first make a deposit, you earn interest just on that amount. But periodically there is interest added onto that, so your account balance increases. You then earn interest on that new, higher amount.

For an interactive example of how compounding interest works, check out the Compounding Calculator at TheMint.org: http://themint.org/tweens/compounding-calculator2.html

---

4

REMEMBER THE RULE OF 72

The "Rule of 72" is a handy little trick that can help you estimate how long it will take for your money to double in an interest-earning account. You divide 72 by the interest rate, and that tells you how long it will take to double your money. For example, if you earn 4 percent interest, it will take you 18 years to double your money.

DIRECT DEPOSIT

It used to be a common sight: on payday, workers would make a trip to the bank to deposit or cash their paychecks. This is why there would often be a long line at banks on Friday afternoons. These days, many employees never actually see a traditional paycheck. That's because a lot of companies pay their employees via direct deposit. This is where the company automatically deposits your pay into your bank account. You don't need to do anything with your paycheck—that money just shows up in your account on payday. One thing to remember: you must make sure your employer always has your current, accurate bank account information. If you switch banks or change your account numbers, your paycheck may not get deposited or it may be delayed.

CHECKING ACCOUNTS

Most people have some type of checking account; this is what they typically use to pay bills and do their routine banking. However, the title is misleading, at least in today's modern banking environment. These days, you often don't even get an actual checkbook when you open a checking account. (And if you do, it may contain only a small number of "starter checks," and you must order a supply if you need more.)

Thanks to the popularity of online banking, people don't write as many checks as they used to. When you open a checking account, you will usually receive an ATM/debit card for the account. This is what many people use in order to do their bill-paying and to spend their money.

We'll cover online banking in more detail shortly.

For now, let's cover the basics of how a checking account works in the traditional sense. When you want to buy something, you write out a check to pay for it. The person or business to which you wrote the check would then deposit or cash it in order to get the money. At that time, if there isn't enough money in your account to cover the check, it may be refused or returned. In other words, it will "bounce." Sometimes, the bank will still honor the check, but then you will have an overdrawn account, meaning your balance will be in the negative. Not only will you have to deposit the amount needed to bring your account into the positive again, but most likely you will also be charged an overdraft fee, which typically is somewhere around $35 or $40 per item. This can become very expensive because banks will often charge a variety of different fees for this situation. For example, they may charge a daily fee for each day your account remains overdrawn. It is also common for banks to impose an "extended overdraft fee," if your account remains overdrawn for a certain period of time (say, a week or ten days). These fees can add up quickly and can become very costly.

Not long ago, it was easy to get a free checking account (meaning, one that doesn't charge monthly fees or maintenance charges). These days, many banks have done away with free checking accounts so that option may be tougher to find. Many banks do still offer "free" checking accounts with a catch—meaning, it's only free if you meet certain conditions, such as maintaining a certain minimum balance or setting up a direct deposit arrangement. So be sure to ask about any rules or restrictions when you open your account.

Most banks offer a selection of different types of checking and savings accounts, each with its own fees, "perks," and rules. Be sure to compare all of the available choices so you can pick the one that's the best fit for you.

How to Write Out a Check

This may seem silly, but many people—especially young people—who have checking accounts rarely (if ever) write out an actual check. That's because they do most of their transactions online or use a debit card.

However, sooner or later, there probably will come a time when you will need to use the old-school method and write out a paper check, so it's a good idea to become familiar with the basic process.

Sample Check

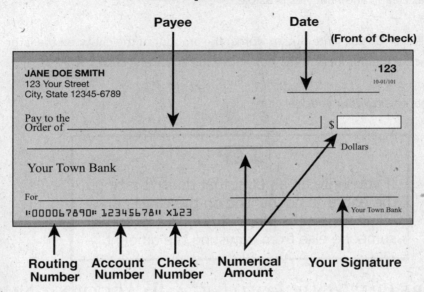

Payee

Date

(Front of Check)

JANE DOE SMITH
123 Your Street
City, State 12345-6789

123

10-01/101

Pay to the
Order of _____

$ ☐

_____ Dollars

Your Town Bank

For_____

⑆000067890⑆ 123456789⑈ X123

Your Town Bank

Routing Number

Account Number

Check Number

Numerical Amount

Your Signature

(Back of Check)

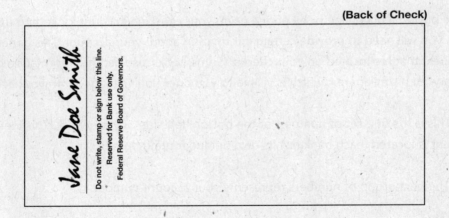

Jane Doe Smith

Do not write, stamp or sign below this line.
Reserved for Bank use only.
Federal Reserve Board of Governors.

Pay to the order of: Since this is the person or business you are paying, you would write their name here. An example of this would be "John Smith" or "Macy's."

Date: This is something people often overlook, but most banks won't process a check if it doesn't have a date. You should use the current date. Most businesses won't accept a post-dated check (meaning, one that is dated for some point in the future).

Numeric amount: Next to the "pay to" line is a line or box where you enter the amount of the check, in numerical digits. Write as clearly and neatly as possible.

Amount (in words): Next, you will write out (in words) the amount of the check on the large line. This is sort of like a backup, in case the numbers in the box above the line aren't clear.

Signature: Don't forget to sign your check!

TIP

If you write an amount that doesn't take up the entire "amount" line on the check, draw a line across the blank space, to prevent someone else from adjusting the amount.

How to Figure Out Your Routing and Account Numbers

Often, when you are paying a bill online or by phone using your checking account, or setting up a direct deposit arrangement, you will need to provide certain information about your account. This generally involves a set of numbers that are located on your checks. (Some banks also list this information online in your "account summary" or a similar area, which is visible to you once you've logged into your account.)

Routing number: This is the first set of numbers at the bottom left side of your check. This identifies the bank where the account is located (each bank has its own unique routing number).

Account number: The next group of numbers represents your account number.

(Note, you won't need to provide this, but the number after your account number is the check number, which should be the same as the number that appears in the upper-right hand corner of the check.)

BALANCING A CHECKBOOK

The phrase "balancing a checkbook" refers to the process of adding up all of your outstanding checks, debits, and other amounts that will be deducted from your account—and then subtracting that number from your current or most recent balance, to figure out exactly how much money you truly have available.

In the past, it could take up to a week or more for checks to "clear" (meaning, for them to be fully processed and the amount to be deducted from your account). This made it very important for you to keep track of the outstanding checks you had. You didn't want to go by the balance currently showing on your account because you might have had one or more checks that hadn't cleared yet.

Balancing your checkbook allows you to see how much money you truly have available to spend, after factoring in any outstanding checks.

Some banks now offer a feature called "remote check capture" (or something similar). This means that if you want to deposit a check, you can do that simply by taking a picture of the check with your phone and submitting it. This is very convenient, as it saves you the time and hassle of making a trip to the bank.

These days, of course, people write fewer paper checks—and checks clear a lot faster (sometimes they are deducted from your account instantly). However, the concept of balancing your account is still important—perhaps more than ever. If you are like many people, you use your debit card to make purchases and, possibly, to make payments online. The amount of time it takes these electronic payments to process can vary widely. Often, electronic payments are processed instantly, but sometimes it can take one to two days—or more.

Checking your account balance online (or via an ATM) can be misleading because you may still have outstanding charges that haven't been processed yet. Therefore, it is very important that you keep careful records of all your transactions. Keep track of what you have spent and charges you have made to your account. Then subtract those from your current balance to determine how much you truly have available.

Note: When you use a debit (or credit) card to make purchases, the store or business sometimes will just put a minimal charge on your account—often it's for $1—just to make sure the card is valid. After the transaction is completed, they will replace this charge with the actual amount of your purchase. However, this may take a few days. If that actual amount isn't available when that time comes, the charge may be refused or your account may become overdrawn.

If you are currently a student and are nearing graduation, check with your bank to see if anything related to your account will change once you are out of school. Often, banks have special types of accounts just for students. Once you graduate, you may then start incurring new fees, or the bank may transition your account to a different type.

Be Prepared for Fast (or Instant) Processing

Before online and electronic banking—when checking accounts operated solely using actual paper checks—it would take a while (usually at least a few days) for a check you wrote to actually be processed so that amount could be deducted from your account. Many people relied on this fact, especially if they were using some strategic timing when their current account balance was low. For example, if you needed groceries on a Thursday night but your pay wasn't going to be deposited until Friday morning, you could be pretty sure that your pay would show up way before the grocery store processed your check. People referred to this cushion of a few days as "the float." (Meaning, your check would be floating around out there for a while before the dollar amount actually came out of your account.)

Times have changed. Now, many stores and other businesses simply scan your check and process it electronically—meaning the bank can deduct that amount instantly from your account. If the funds aren't available to cover your check, you may incur overdraft fees and other charges—or your transaction may simply be denied. Bottom line: be careful to write out checks only if you know you have the funds in your account to cover that amount right at that time.

Beware of Fees

Banks can (and often do) charge fees for a wide variety of things, and it seems like they are always coming up with creative new fees to impose on customers. Obviously, there are the old standards like overdraft fees, and monthly "maintenance fees" are also common (and seem to be getting larger). But now, some banks charge fees for things like getting a paper bank statement or checking your balance at an ATM. In the case of a checking account, you may not even get any paper checks from the beginning unless you are willing to pay for them. These fees can really add up, and, if your account has a very low balance, the fees can even cause it to become overdrawn. So be sure to research any fees your bank charges—and if you see a fee on your statement that you don't recognize, ask your bank about it.

10

DEBIT CARDS

Virtually all checking accounts (and many savings accounts) will provide you with a debit card. Basically, this is an ATM card that also can be used to make purchases at stores or online. We will discuss debit cards in more detail in Chapter Five.

ONLINE BANKING AND BILL PAYING

Many people conduct a lot of their banking business and financial transactions without ever going anywhere near a bank. These days, you can take care of many of your money-related tasks from your computer (or even your smartphone).

You actually might be surprised at the kinds of things you can pay online. You can pay your taxes, make your car insurance payment, and pay your cell phone and other utility bills, too. Most likely, you can pay your college tuition or other school-related bills online. Also, you can use PayPal or other online payment services to pay for eBay purchases, send money to friends, or to make an online payment to many places.

Most (if not all) major banks offer online banking. However, the specific features and setup can vary widely, as can any fees that may be associated with some online transactions.

Even if you don't use online banking, there is one aspect you should use: the alerts feature. Most banks with online banking give you the option of setting up various types of alerts. These alerts will send you an e-mail or text message if a certain thing happens—for example, if there is an electronic withdrawal from your account, if a charge is made that exceeds a certain amount, or if your account balance falls below a specific amount. These alerts can help you avoid overdraft charges and other fees, or they can clue you in that some sort of suspicious or unauthorized activity has occurred.

11

KEEP ALERT FOR SIGNS OF TROUBLE

One of the best advantages of online banking is that it lets you monitor your account 24/7, and you can see most activity in real time, as it happens (or very soon after). This lets you spot anything suspicious or inaccurate immediately. You should check your account activity often—get in the habit of doing it on a daily basis. Keep an eye out for any charges you don't recognize or signs of anything strange—for example, if there's a pending charge from a business you don't know or from a location you haven't been. If you spot anything, notify your bank right away. Depending on the circumstances, the bank may need to freeze or close your account, or cancel your card, to avoid any more problems. They will then open a new account for you using different numbers.

IMPORTANT THINGS TO KEEP IN MIND ABOUT ONLINE BANKING

Online banking and bill paying can be very convenient, and they can save you a lot of time. But there are a few things to remember:

- Be very careful about providing your account numbers (or any other personal information) online. Only provide your information to businesses and sites you know and trust. And never click on links in an e-mail—they're often fake sites set up by hackers and scam artists. (We will discuss this more in Chapter Eight.)
- While the bank processes many transactions instantly—or at least very quickly—that is not always the case. Be sure to read the terms and conditions, or any fine print, about the standard processing time for transactions. This is especially important if you are paying a bill at the last minute, because if the transaction isn't processed right away, your payment may actually be considered late.

STUDY YOUR BANK STATEMENT

You will normally get a statement from your bank once a month that lists all of the transactions for your account that occurred throughout that month. Most banks now offer paperless statements, so you may not actually get a paper statement in the mail—it may just be available for you to access online.

Depending on your bank—and the volume of transactions you have—a monthly bank statement can be long and may seem intimidating at first, with so many figures and abbreviations. But it's important for you to review it as soon as possible, so that you know exactly how much is available in your account. This also lets you spot any suspicious activity, as well as any mistakes on the bank's part.

Of course, if you use online banking and get in the habit of checking your account activity on a daily basis—or at least as often as possible—it should be fairly easy for you to review your monthly statement quickly because you will have already seen most of the transactions listed there.

TYPES OF BANKS

There are different kinds of banks these days: traditional banks, credit unions, and online only. Here is some information to help you sort this out.

TRADITIONAL BANKS

A traditional bank is just a standard, old-fashioned type of bank—the kind your parents or grandparents may have always used. You go into a local branch of the bank and make deposits and withdrawals or whatever other business you need. There are tellers there to take care of you, and you can talk to a customer service representative or branch manager if you need help.

Many traditional banks offer some high-tech services. For example, they may have a mobile app that lets you check your balance and conduct certain transactions from your phone or other mobile device. And of course, a lot of them do offer online banking, so you can conduct your business from your computer.

13

CREDIT UNIONS

You have to be a member of a credit union in order to do business there. The good news is, there are lots of different types of credit unions, so there's a good chance that there are at least a few in your area that you can join.

Some credit unions are only available for a certain community, so if you live within their geographic area, you can join. Others are tied to a certain industry, employer, or organization. For example, there are credit unions specifically for people who work for certain government agencies or for people who are members of certain labor unions. Often, if a member of your household or family is eligible to become a member, then you can join as well.

HOW A CREDIT UNION IS DIFFERENT FROM A BANK

In many ways, credit unions and banks are similar. They both deal with the same basic types of financial transactions: deposits, withdrawals, loans, and so on. However, there are a few major differences:

- A board of directors runs a credit union, which is a nonprofit organization. In addition, there's a democratic process, which gives members a say in the operation of the organization. For example, when there are board elections, each account holder gets a vote, no matter how much money is in his or her account.
- Fees, loan rates, and other charges are often lower at a credit union than at a bank.
- Since credit unions are nonprofit, they pass any earnings back to their members in the form of better rates.
- Because credit unions tend to be smaller than banks and have a community-based focus, some people say the service is better and there's a more personal touch than at large banks.

ONLINE-ONLY BANKS

A category of banks that is relatively new—but growing quickly—is online-only banks. As you can guess by the name, these banks conduct all of their business online. There are no actual bank locations staffed by tellers. If you are a customer at an online-only bank, you can, of course, still use your ATM/debit card at a regular ATM machine.

14

Online-only banks often charge fewer (and lower) fees than traditional banks. This is because online-only banks have less overhead—since they don't have buildings to maintain—so they can pass those savings along to their customers.

There are pros and cons of using online-only banks. One nice thing is that, by their nature, they were designed for the tech-savvy consumer, so they tend to have the latest high-tech bells and whistles, like cool apps and other tools. In addition, they tend to have lower/fewer fees than traditional banks.

On the downside, obviously you can't go into an actual office and sit down to talk with someone if you have a question or concern. In addition, online banks typically have a smaller network of ATMs, meaning you may be more likely to incur fees if you have to use another bank's ATM.

If you decide to go with an online bank, be sure to pick one that the FDIC insures. That means you will have the same protection against loss as you would at a traditional bank. You can use the FDIC's BankFind tool (http://research.fdic.gov/bankfind/) to locate FDIC-insured banking institutions.

DECIDING WHICH BANK TO USE

Think about all of the banks in your town or neighborhood. Chances are there are quite a few of them. Then, when you add on credit unions (not to mention online-only banks), there are many choices! So how do you know which one to choose?

You don't want to just pick one at random, because there are a lot of differences—and lots of things you should consider.

Some people like to deal with local community banks, which tend to be smaller and often focus on a more individual, personal touch. To find a community bank, download The Independent Community Bankers of America's (ICBA) app, a free locator of community banks. You just enter your zip code, and the ICBA locator app will show you all the community banks in your area. Visit: http://www.icba.org/locate.

THINGS TO CONSIDER

Your Banking Habits and Preferences: Do you often need to ask questions about your banking issues, or do you often need assistance from a bank employee? Then a traditional bank that allows you to conduct in-person business is probably the best fit. If, on the other hand, you rarely—if ever—actually go to a bank location and conduct all of your transactions online, then an online-only bank may be fine for you.

Locations and Availability: If you do choose a brick-and-mortar bank, be sure it has locations that are convenient to you, so you don't waste lots of time (and gas money) traveling to the nearest branch to conduct your business.

Fees: This is an important consideration. Banks charge fees for all sorts of things, and those fees can really add up. If you are considering opening an account at a bank or credit union, be sure to research all of their fees beforehand to see what kind of charges you might incur. And don't forget to investigate fees that people often overlook—such as a fee you might be charged for using an ATM that's not in the bank's network.

Size of the Bank and Its Network: If you will need to visit the bank in person often or use an ATM frequently, a larger/national bank may be a better fit for you, as you will have more locations from which to choose. Having a bank that's part of a large network makes it more likely that you will be able to find an ATM without incurring an extra fee.

Reputation and Customer Service: This is especially important if you anticipate needing help often. You want a bank that treats its customers well and has a good reputation for handling problems or questions promptly and courteously. Fortunately, it's very easy to find out about a bank's reputation and track record—a quick Internet search will turn up any reports or bad reviews from unhappy customers.

Sometimes colleges have relationships/partnerships with specific banks, so students of that school will get special "perks" or advantages if they have an account with that bank. Check your school's website to see if it promotes any specific banks.

IMPORTANT THINGS TO REMEMBER

- There are several different types of banks, and each offers a number of different types of accounts. Do your research so you can select the bank and account that will work best for you. You can usually get this information on the bank's website.

- It's important to keep a close eye on your account activity to be able to spot any mistakes or suspicious items.

- Stay organized and carefully record of all your transactions, so you know exactly how much money you have available. Don't rely on the balance that is displayed on the ATM receipt, as you may still have other transactions that haven't cleared yet.

- Be sure to find out about any fees a bank may charge on your account. Even small fees can really add up.

CHAPTER TWO: ESTABLISHING A FINANCIAL IDENTITY

Just like anything else, when it comes to establishing a financial identity, you have to start somewhere—and the sooner, the better. You don't develop a financial identity overnight. It takes a while for you to establish a good track record and show a history of paying bills on time and managing credit responsibly.

In the world of credit and banking, you generally have to start out with small amounts and then gradually move up. Most likely, your bank accounts will involve small amounts at first. You may even feel a bit silly setting up an account just to keep this small amount of money in it. However, this is good practice, so that you will be comfortable handling banking tasks. It will also help get you in the habit of saving money when the time comes that you have more money to worry about. Also, if you have an interest-earning account, the little bit of money with which you start out can grow quickly. Likewise, you may be a bit discouraged that your first credit account will probably have a relatively low limit. But again, this is a good "training period" to help you get comfortable with the process.

More important, you are establishing a history. Your credit report and credit score (which we will discuss in a later chapter) use a formula in which the length of your credit record carries considerable weight. The longer you have had credit, the better. Even if you don't think you will need credit or a bank account right now, it is to your benefit to open these accounts as early as possible.

Another advantage to opening a bank account—even a small one—is that it lets you establish a relationship with that bank, through which the employees will get to know you. This makes it much easier for you to then get other services or conduct other business there. For example, it is usually much easier to cash a check at a bank where you have an account. In addition, banks may offer better terms (or easier approval) to people who are already customers of the bank. This is why it may be to your advantage to conduct business in-person at the bank occasionally (even if you could do your business online or at an ATM), because then the staff will start to recognize you.

WHERE TO START

What's the best way to get started with your financial activity? Generally, a basic checking or savings account is the easiest place to start out when you don't have a lot of financial experience. Look for a free account that has as few charges as possible. Obviously, you will want to look for an account that has no minimum balance—or, at least, a low minimum balance.

You should make sure this initial account offers online banking, so that you can get some practice in using that type of system and become comfortable keeping track of your account activity.

For a credit account, you will probably begin with a low-limit account. That's okay—it will give you access to credit and the opportunity to start building a credit history, without the ability to rack up charges that are too high.

You don't want to make the mistake of rushing out and charging this card to the limit right off the bat. For one thing, you'll run the risk of going over your limit, which hurts your credit and can also result in an over-limit fee.

Here's another reason to avoid maxing out your first credit card: the formula for calculating your credit score considers the ratio of how much credit you use compared to how much you have available. Ideally, you want to keep most of your available credit unused. A good strategy is to make a small charge on the card— say, by using it at the gas station or for the movies—and then immediately pay off that balance by the due date. This way, you will avoid any interest charges while still showing a history of responsible credit card use.

If you have difficulty getting even a low-limit credit card, you may need to start with a secured account. (We'll discuss those in more detail in Chapter Five.) While this isn't the ideal option, it's still an effective way to get started. Often your secured account will later be transitioned into a regular charge account once you've maintained it in good standing for a certain period of time.

EXPERT ADVICE

"The student can become an authorized user on his or her parents' credit card account. I often coach parents, that when the student is going off to college, to have the first credit card be equipped with parental control on the card—meaning, the card is in the parent's name with the student being an authorized user on the card."

Kimberly Foss, CFP, personal finance expert and president of Empyrion Wealth Management in Roseville, California

OPENING YOUR FIRST ACCOUNTS

Opening your first accounts may be a more time-consuming process than you will experience when you open any subsequent accounts. This is because the bank or credit company will need to verify your identity and may need to check your credit or bank history; this could take some time.

BANK ACCOUNTS

When you open your first bank account, you will need to fill out some paperwork. You will also need to prove your identity. Generally, banks require two forms of identification. One of these must be a picture ID, such as a driver's license or a type of government identification card. (A school ID card might not be acceptable as the primary identification but probably could be a secondary form of ID.) The banker probably will also want to see something that shows your current address.

21

A bank doesn't automatically allow you to open an account. When you request an account, bank representatives will usually check your bank record. This is different from a credit check. The bank is looking to see if you have a history of negative activity at other banks, such as repeatedly bouncing checks or incurring overdraft charges. If this is the case, the bank can refuse to let you open an account.

When you first open an account, the bank will require you to make an initial deposit. Some banks have a minimum amount for an opening deposit, but other banks will let you to deposit whatever amount you wish.

At some banks, there are certain limitations on services or benefits available for new account holders. For example, your deposits may not clear quite as quickly or you may not get fees that are quite as favorable. Once you've passed a certain milestone and you have an established account, you will get the same treatment as other account holders.

CREDIT ACCOUNTS

When you open your first credit account (or apply for your first loan), your biggest challenge will be that you lack any sort of credit history or track record. Having no credit record is almost as bad as having poor credit from the viewpoint of a bank or business that is considering granting you credit. The fact that you are unproven—in terms of showing you can manage credit responsibly—makes you a higher risk in their eyes.

Most likely, you will have to start out with a very small limit for your first account. Don't be discouraged—if you prove that you can manage this account well, your limit will likely be increased fairly quickly.

To open your first credit account, you will need to complete a credit application. This will ask you to provide some personal information, such as your social security number, birth date, and other data. You will also need to provide information about your employer and income—the creditor wants to be sure you have enough income to pay the bill without a problem.

For a loan application, the lender may also need information about the item you will be purchasing with the loan. In the case of a loan to finance a vehicle or property, the lender may need additional information or documentation about that item (for example, an appraisal for a home or other real estate), because it will be used to secure the loan. This means the lender will put a lien on the vehicle or property until the borrower pays it off.

22

SHOULD YOU GET A CO-SIGNER?

In some cases, if the bank feels you don't have a sufficient credit history (or if you have some negative items on your credit report), the lender may want you to enlist a co-signer. This is most common in the case of a personal loan or a loan to buy a car or real estate.

A co-signer is someone who agrees to be responsible for that debt, in the event you fail to make payments. This is the lender's assurance that they will not be stuck with an unpaid loan because someone—either you or your co-signer—will have to pay it.

While obviously this isn't the ideal scenario for you, it may be your only option if you want the loan. The good news is that this will still be an account in your name. Once you pay it off successfully, your credit picture will improve, and you will probably be able to then get a loan or credit on your own merit, without a co-signer.

Asking someone to co-sign a loan for you is a major step. Many people are uncomfortable or unwilling to sign a loan for someone else, and you will be putting them on the spot by asking them. This may make for an awkward situation. For this reason, many loan applicants just tell the lender they aren't interested in any loan that requires a co-signer.

Whether or not you would consider asking someone to co-sign a loan for you is your own personal decision. Keep in mind, though, that this person will be on the hook for your debt should you be unable to pay it. Obviously, you would want to give this a lot of thought and be sure you're comfortable asking someone to take on that obligation.

HOW TO GET THE MOST BENEFIT FROM YOUR FIRST ACCOUNTS

Once you have obtained your first bank or credit accounts, you want to best use them to help with your long-term strategy of establishing a good financial identity. Here are some tips that will help:

- In the case of credit accounts, be sure they report to the national credit bureaus. (Most of the major credit companies do report to those bureaus, but some smaller retailers or companies may not.) As a result, your positive credit activities will show up on your credit report and will help improve your credit score.

- Be sure to avoid overdrafts or exceeding your credit limit. You don't want any negative items to appear on your record.

- Once you have maintained an account in good standing for a while, ask about getting additional "perks" or obtaining a high credit limit.

SECOND CHANCE CHECKING ACCOUNTS

Did you make a few money mistakes in the past? If it involved a checking account, there may be ways to help you recover from your past missteps. If you previously had a checking account that a bank closed (let's say it was because you had repeated overdrafts), you may have trouble opening an account with another bank through the normal process. That's because, as we mentioned before, banks often do a routine banking background check when you try to open an account.

TIP

Wells Fargo has an Opportunity Package (https://www.wellsfargo.com/checking/opportunity/), which is a bundle of banking services designed for people who have trouble getting bank accounts due to poor banking, poor credit history, or both.

However, you aren't totally out of luck. Some banks offer "second chance" checking accounts to people who have had banking issues in the past. Because you are more of a risk to the bank, these accounts often have higher monthly fees or involve other restrictions. However, compared to the fees you would pay at check-cashing places or the costs for other services you might need if you lack a bank account, these fees could end up saving you money. On the plus side, the bank will often allow you to get a regular account once you've maintained this "second chance" account in good standing for a specified period of time.

IMPORTANT THINGS TO REMEMBER

Opening a bank or credit account for the first time may be more time consuming and require more paperwork than for subsequent accounts.

• You will need to provide proof of your identity—most likely including a photo ID—in order to open a bank or credit account.

• Banks and credit companies will do various types of background checks on you when you first try to open an account. If these reports show negative items, the bank or credit company may deny your application.

• New accounts—especially those for people with little or no credit history—often have low limits, but they can be a good way to establish a financial track record.

CHAPTER THREE: PAYING FOR COLLEGE

If you are currently in college (or are preparing to go there soon), most of your financial decisions and challenges right now probably relate to school. College is expensive—and tuition and other costs continue to soar—so trying to manage these school-related expenses can be a real challenge.

That's why it is so important to do your research—and start as early as possible. There are various options available to help you pay for school, but many of them have steps that must be followed far in advance of the first day of class. And there are applications and other paperwork that must be completed. This can be a complicated and time-consuming process. Waiting until the last minute might cause you to rush and overlook important details that could have a negative impact on your financial aid.

HOW MUCH WILL IT ACTUALLY COST?

Of course, you can't try to come up with a plan of how you will pay for school until you know how much money you will need. To figure that out, you need to know exactly how much school will cost. This may not be as easy as it seems, because there are several things you need to consider. First, there is the tuition, which often is not a flat fee. So you may need to estimate how many credits you will be taking and then do the math to come up with an estimate. (Some schools have different per-credit rates depending on your program of study or whether you're a freshman or senior.)

Then you must add on the cost of housing, meal plan, and other living expenses. Of course, there are also additional expenses like books, supplies, transportation, and other costs. After that, you must deduct any scholarships, financial aid, and other assistance you may get that will help pay the costs.

Once you are done with all of these calculations, you will have an estimate of your bottom line—meaning, the amount you will need to pay out of your own pocket. As you will see, this could be much different from the initial "sticker price" figure with which you started.

Colleges are now required to have "net price" calculators available online on their websites. This tool helps you estimate your actual cost of attendance. However, the thoroughness and accuracy of these calculators can vary widely, so while it's nice to give it a try, don't consider the results to be a completely accurate figure.

SAVING FOR COLLEGE

If you are already in college, you know how expensive it is. It's never too late, though, to save money for upcoming years of your higher education.

529 PLANS

529 Savings Plans (the name comes from the section of the IRS tax code that regulates these plans) are a way for your parents or other relatives to help you save money for college. You can also open a 529 Plan yourself to save up for your college bills. These plans offer several tax benefits:

- The money you put into the plan isn't subject to federal or state taxes.
- Your investment grows tax-free while it is in the account.
- You don't pay federal taxes on any money you withdraw for qualified educational expenses; in many states, withdrawals are also exempt from state taxes.

It doesn't take a lot of money to start or maintain a 529 Plan. Usually, you can start the account with a small contribution, and then there generally is a low monthly minimum.

You don't have to choose the plan offered by your state. Most states allow you to invest in their plan no matter where you live, but you may get extra state tax benefits for investing in the plan of the state where you are a resident. You can use the money from your plan to pay for expenses at virtually any accredited college or secondary school in the country (and even some overseas), regardless of where you actually live.

There is no one plan that is best for everyone—your family's individual situation and goals will determine which plan(s) would be the best fit for you. SavingForCollege.com has a comprehensive guide to 529 Plans, with a breakdown of specific plans by state.
Check out http://www.savingforcollege.com/college_savings_101/ for more information.

FINANCIAL AID

Many (probably most) college students and their families count on—or at least hope for—financial aid to help with the cost of attending school. Financial aid can come in many forms, including grants, scholarships, loans, and even work-study jobs. The process of applying for financial aid can take some time and work, so you should start doing your research and become familiar with the process as early as possible.

FAFSA

The Free Application for Federal Student Aid (FAFSA) is very important if you want to get financial aid. This form is required in order to apply for any government-related financial aid (grants or loans).

You can complete the FAFSA online at http://www.fafsa.ed.gov/.

You will want to complete the FAFSA as early as possible. There are deadlines for each financial aid program, and if you miss them, you will be out of luck. Also, some financial aid programs have a limited amount of funds so they are awarded on a first-come, first-served basis. So if you wait too long, the funds may already be gone.

You can complete the FAFSA for the upcoming school year starting on January 1. You will need your financial information (ideally, your tax returns), as well as those of your parents, if you are considered a dependent student. We'll discuss the issue of dependency in more detail later in this chapter.

It is completely free to submit the FAFSA. (Watch out for other websites that want to charge you to complete the FAFSA!)

TIP

In order to complete the FAFSA, you will need to obtain a federal Student Aid PIN, which you can get for free online at http://www.pin.ed.gov/. If you are a dependent student, your parents will also need to get a PIN of their own, since they will need to provide some of their information for your FAFSA.

29

CSS/Financial Aid PROFILE

The other common financial aid application form is the CSS/Financial Aid Profile® (PROFILE). Many private colleges use this form to award non-federal financial aid. Unlike the FAFSA, the PROFILE may be submitted before January 1, is not free to submit, and is very detailed.

The PROFILE (http://student.collegeboard.org/css-financial-aid-profile) asks for much more information than the FAFSA and considers financial information that the FAFSA does not. However, completing this form can really be beneficial, as some private schools award a considerable amount of money in scholarships and aid—and the amount of aid students receive from these schools is determined by the information that students provide in the PROFILE form.

Additional Forms

In addition to the FAFSA and CSS PROFILE, some schools have their own supplemental forms that students must complete in order to apply for financial aid from the school. Be sure to ask the financial aid office about any forms you need to complete—and make sure you are very clear about the deadlines.

EFC—Expected Family Contribution

Your EFC is perhaps the most important number in your financial aid process. The EFC (Expected Family Contribution) is the government's way of determining how much your family can pay for your college expenses. The higher the EFC, the less chance you have of financial aid. The information you and your parents provide when you submit your application for federal financial aid (FAFSA) determines your EFC. It is a complicated process to calculate the EFC—as illustrated by the 36-page-long Department of Education explanation of the EFC formula for the 2013–14 academic year, which can be found at http://ifap.ed.gov/efcformulaguide/attachments/091312EFCFormulaGuide1314.pdf. However, there are several online EFC estimators that can help you get a rough (and unofficial) estimate of your EFC.

DON'T BE MISLED BY THE EFC!

It's important to remember that the EFC is not necessarily the amount you actually will pay to attend school (unfortunately, most students end up paying a lot more than that figure), and it is also not the amount of financial aid you will get. The EFC is simply a figure that the government and colleges use in determining financial aid eligibility and calculating financial aid awards.

YOU COULD HAVE MORE THAN ONE EFC

The government will use the FAFSA to determine your EFC for federal financial aid. However, colleges often have their own formula to determine aid eligibility, so—depending on what type of formula the college uses—it may come up with a different EFC to use to determine the amount of aid you will be able to receive.

THINGS THAT AFFECT YOUR EFC

Financial aid forms require a lot of figures and other financial information. Then, someone plugs the data into a formula to calculate the EFC. Here are some of the main factors that affect your EFC:

- **Income:** This has a major impact on your EFC. The student's income is "weighted" more heavily than his or her parents. This is because the government assumes that your parents must use their income to support the entire household, and their available money is divided up into paying for several people—whereas you can use all of your income for your own expenses.

- **Marital status:** The marital status of the student (or, for dependent students, parents) is a very important part of the EFC formula. If a student is married, he or she is considered independent automatically—meaning his or her parents' information is irrelevant. In the case of dependent students, the parents' marital status can determine whether their information is considered. (This varies depending on the form; for example, on the FAFSA, if a student's parents are divorced, only the primary parent's information is considered.)

While most of the data you enter in your FAFSA is from the previous calendar year, marital status is an exception. Marital status must be accurate at the time you complete the form. So if you (or your parent) recently got married or divorced, you would use that status on your FAFSA, even if it's different from your status for the previous calendar year.

- **Assets:** These also are taken into account. It's worth noting that for the FAFSA, if you own your primary home (the one you live in), that isn't considered one of your assets. In addition, you can have a certain amount of education savings and assets that are considered "protected" and are not factored into your EFC calculation. This amount is determined by the age of your older parent.

- **Household size:** The number of people in your household is considered. However, you must read the instructions on the financial aid form carefully, as there are specific rules as to who qualifies as an official member of the household.

- **Number of students in college:** The more household members are in college, the lower your EFC will be. (Note: You aren't allowed to include your parents in this number, even if they are in college.)

- **Parental age:** If you are a dependent student, your older parent's age is considered in determining how much of the assets will be factored into the formula.

THINGS THAT DON'T AFFECT YOUR EFC

- **Expenses and cost of living:** People who have a high mortgage or live in an area with a high cost of living often think those factors should be taken into consideration when evaluating their financial aid, but your household expenses and cost of living are irrelevant to your EFC.

- **Grades:** Your grades are not considered when calculating your EFC. However, you do need to maintain Satisfactory Academic Progress (explained later) in order to remain eligible for financial aid. In addition, many scholarships require you to maintain a certain GPA or otherwise maintain certain academic standards.

An easy way to estimate your EFC, and to see how certain adjustments to your situation may affect your EFC, is to use an EFC estimator, such as the one on FinAid.org.

ARE YOU A DEPENDENT STUDENT?

Dependency status is something that often confuses people. There are also some common misconceptions about who is (or can become) an independent student.

Dependent/independent status can make a big difference when it comes to financial aid. If you are a dependent student, your parents' financial information, and possibly even that of their new spouse(s), if they have been remarried, will be used as part of the formula to determine your EFC. The formula assumes they will contribute toward your educational costs, and it doesn't matter if they can or are willing to do so.

Years ago, it was easier to change one's dependency status. A student could simply get his or her own apartment, and he or she then would be considered independent. These days, there are specific criteria that one must meet to be considered independent.

It's important to remember that dependency for the purposes of financial aid has nothing to do with tax-related dependent status. It doesn't matter whether or not your parents claim you as a dependent on their tax return. Unless you meet the criteria to be classified as an independent student, which we'll explain next, you are considered a dependent student.

This information, courtesy of the Department of Education, explains how the government determines if you are a dependent student:

For the 2013–14 award year, a student is automatically determined to be an **independent applicant** for federal student aid if he or she meets one or more of the following criteria:

- The student was born before January 1, 1990.

- The student is married or separated (but not divorced) as of the date of the application.

- At the beginning of the school year, the student will be enrolled in a master's or doctoral degree program.

- The student is currently serving on active duty in the U.S. Armed Forces or is a National Guard or Reserves enlistee called into federal active duty for other than training purposes.

- The student is a veteran of the U.S. Armed Forces.

- The student has one or more children who receive more than half of their support from him or her between July 1, 2013 and June 30, 2014.

- The student has dependent(s) (other than children or spouse) who live with him or her and who receive more than half of their support from the student, now and through June 30, 2014.

- At any time since the student turned age 13, both of the student's parents were deceased, the student was in foster care, or the student was a dependent/ward of the court.

- As determined by a court in the student's state of legal residence, the student is now or was upon reaching the age of majority, an emancipated minor (released from control by his or her parent or guardian).

- As determined by a court in the student's state of legal residence, the student is now or was upon reaching the age of majority, in legal guardianship.

- On or after July 1, 2012, a high school or school district homeless liaison determined that the student was an unaccompanied youth who was homeless.

- On or after July 1, 2012, the director of an emergency shelter or transitional housing program funded by the U.S. Department of Housing and Urban Development determined that the student was an unaccompanied youth who was homeless.

- On or after July 1, 2012, a director of a runaway or homeless youth basic center or transitional living program determined that the student was an unaccompanied youth who was homeless or was self-supporting and at risk of being homeless.

- The college financial aid administrator determined that the student was an unaccompanied youth who is homeless or is self-supporting and at risk of being homeless.

The answers you provide on the FAFSA and other financial aid forms will determine your dependency status. Since the criteria are very clear cut, the system will easily determine your dependency status based upon your answers to a few quick questions.

If you disagree with your dependency status, you would need to request a dependency override or appeal. However, it is usually quite challenging to get a dependency status changed. Appeals that have the best chance of success tend to involve students who have been on their own for a long time because their parents have been completely absent, perhaps because of incarceration or substance abuse problems.

COULD YOU GET AN AUTOMATIC ZERO EFC?

If you meet specific criteria, you may qualify for an automatic EFC of zero. Students who meet certain criteria, such as having an income under a certain amount, may qualify for an automatic zero EFC. Details about how to qualify are listed on the Department of Education website http://ifap.ed.gov/efcformulaguide/attachments/091312EFCFormulaGuide1314.pdf, or they can be provided by your school's financial aid office.

IF YOU EXPERIENCE A CRISIS OR FINANCIAL EMERGENCY

Here's something you may not know: the financial aid officers at your school (or potential school) have the ability to change your EFC. This is through a process called Professional Judgment, which is a special circumstances review. Technically, the financial aid officer doesn't change the actual EFC. Instead, the officer changes one or more of the figures, or data elements, which are used in the EFC formula—such as the figure for your income, assets, or medical expenses. This, in turn, results in a change to the EFC.

You can't ask for this review just because you feel your EFC is unfair. (If that were the case, almost every parent or student would request it.) There must be some extenuating circumstances—say, if a parent dies, if a parent has been unemployed for an extended period of time, or if your family has substantial medical bills.

35

The school will usually have a policy as to how and when you can request a review. For example, in the case of a job loss, the student/parent may need to be out of work for at least several months.

You can usually find out more information about the circumstances for which your school may consider a professional review on the school's financial aid website or by calling the school's student aid office.

The law requires financial aid administrators to review professional judgment requests on a case-by-case basis. In other words, they cannot just make a blanket policy—for example, they cannot decide that everyone whose parent lost a job will automatically get their EFC reduced by a certain amount (or reduced at all). The good news is that this means your request will get individual attention. The bad news is that the process can take a while. Usually, a committee reviews the request and makes a recommendation.

To start the process, you usually need to complete a form requesting a professional review, sometimes called an appeal form. The specific process varies from school to school. You will need to provide documentation or other proof of your circumstances.

Keep in mind, professional judgment review is usually a "one per customer" type of thing. Once you've gone through the process for one year, you usually cannot request it again another year. So plan wisely. If you suspect your circumstances will become even more challenging in the near future (for example, if you may be laid off soon from your job), you might want to wait and save this opportunity to use during the next school year.

Remember, as with any other financial aid documents you submit, any information you provide must be true. Lying or providing false information is fraud and can get you in big trouble.

DON'T ASSUME A SCHOOL IS OUT OF YOUR REACH FINANCIALLY!

A common mistake many students (and parents) make is to dismiss certain schools automatically as unrealistic, financially speaking, because they assume they won't be able to afford the cost.

However, don't be scared away by a high sticker price. Remember, the official cost is not necessarily what you will have to pay. You must factor in any aid the school will give you, and, in the case of some private schools with big endowment funds, this could be a lot. This is especially true if you are a top-notch student or are in an under-represented demographic at that school.

In addition, being a (financially) poor student can be an advantage in some cases. Some private schools—including Ivy League colleges—have a need-based policy, meaning that families with incomes under a certain amount automatically qualify for full (or nearly full) financial aid. This is generally because the school wants to give the appearance of working toward more financial diversity. Increasingly, these top-tier schools have also been implementing a no-loans system for students from certain income levels—meaning, they will put together a financial aid package that allows you to afford their school without taking out any loans.

To help students save money on college costs, there is a program that can help them earn some of their credits affordably online. **DreamDegree.org** is a student advocacy, not-for-profit organization created to help students achieve their goal of earning a college degree. It also provides information about low tuition and scholarship offers. In addition, personal education coaches are available to help students chart their paths from courses to take to graduation and onto a career, and the free coaching sessions can help students explore alternatives so they can choose the best one.

Low tuition rates offered by **DreamDegree.org** for their online classes can empower students to achieve their goal of an undergraduate degree, whether they're returning to college or attending for the first time.

SATISFACTORY ACADEMIC PROGRESS

In order to maintain eligibility for financial aid, a student must meet what is called Satisfactory Academic Progress (SAP). Federal regulations require schools to establish a policy to ensure students make sufficient progress toward earning their degree. The schools are then also required to monitor students' progress to ensure they are meeting those standards.

There are two components to meeting SAP:

1. **Academic performance:** You must maintain grades of at least a certain level. The Department of Education rules state: "If a student is enrolled in an educational program of more than two academic years, the policy specifies that at the end of the second academic year, the student must have a GPA of at least a "C" or its equivalent, or have academic standing consistent with the school's requirements for graduation."

37

2. **Timeframe:** You must also be moving along at an acceptable rate. (This is to prevent students from taking endless classes simply in an attempt to keep receiving financial aid.) The SAP policy requires you to complete your academic program within a certain timeframe. The Department of Education rules state, "For an undergraduate program measured in credit hours, the maximum timeframe cannot be longer than 150 percent of the published length of the educational program, as measured in credit hours. For an undergraduate program measured in clock hours, the maximum timeframe cannot be longer than 150 percent of the published length of the educational program, as measured by the cumulative number of clock hours the student is required to complete and expressed in calendar time. For a graduate program, the maximum timeframe must be defined by the school and must be based on the length of the educational program."

    [Source: http://ifap.ed.gov/fsahandbook/attachments/1314Vol1Ch1.pdf]

As part of the "acceptable progress" aspect of the policy, you must complete a certain percentage of the classes you attempt. This means you may run into problems if you frequently register for classes but later drop them or withdraw from them once the semester starts.

If you fail to maintain Satisfactory Academic Progress, you may be ineligible to receive financial aid until you improve your academic standing. Usually, this means you will need to pay for at least one semester on your own—without financial aid—so that you can raise your GPA or otherwise satisfy your school's requirements.

Sometimes schools will give you a warning or put you on "financial probation" if they feel you are close to dropping below SAP standards.

NEED-BASED VS. MERIT-BASED AID

Some financial aid programs are need-based. This means your financial need, as established by your EFC, determines whether you are eligible for aid, and, if so, for how much. Most government grants fall into the need-based category.

A few government sources of aid are not needs based: Direct Unsubsidized loans, PLUS loans, and the TEACH grant, for example.

Other aid is merit-based. This would include scholarships that schools award based on a particular skill, athletic participation, academic criteria, or other factors unrelated to finances.

OTHER FACTORS AFFECTING HOW MUCH AID YOU RECEIVE

Your EFC is just one of several factors that your school will use in determining how much aid (if any) you may be eligible to receive. Here are a few other factors that may play a role:

- **Cost of attendance:** This is the school's rough estimate of how much it will cost you to attend that college. It includes tuition and fees, as well as room and board, books and supplies, plus transportation and other expenses.

- **Enrollment status:** Are you enrolled part-time, full-time, or neither? The specific criteria for enrollment status can vary from one school to another, but generally, you must be taking at least 11 or 12 credits per semester for full-time enrollment status.

- **Grade level:** Some aid programs are only available to students at certain grade levels. In many cases, there is a limit as to how long you can be eligible for financial aid. For example, many aid programs are only available to students who have not yet completed their first bachelor's degree.

WHY YOU SHOULD ALWAYS COMPLETE THE FAFSA

Even if you think you will not qualify for need-based aid—perhaps because your household income is too high—you should still complete the FAFSA. For one thing, many scholarships require you to complete this form. In addition, you cannot obtain federal student loans until you have completed the FAFSA. Since it can take a while for the FAFSA to be processed and for the results to be forwarded to your school, you don't want to be scrambling at the last minute to try and take care of it. It is much better to complete the FAFSA early in the year, so the information will be ready and available.

GRANTS

Grants are one of the best forms of financial aid because, unlike loans, they don't have to be paid back. And, whereas scholarships often require you to "jump through a lot of hoops," the application process for grants is usually quite simple. In the case of federal grants, basically, you just complete the FAFSA.

Students receive most grants on a need-based system, so they qualify based on their financial situation, as determined by their EFC. Some grants have additional criteria.

PELL GRANT

The Pell Grant is the main federal grant program available to students with financial need. If you are eligible, several factors determine the amount of the grant you will actually get, including your EFC and whether you are in school on a full-time or part-time basis. For the 2013–14 school year, the maximum Pell Grant a student can receive is $5,635. Keep in mind that only the very neediest of students receive that maximum amount.

FEDERAL SUPPLEMENTAL EDUCATIONAL OPPORTUNITY GRANT (FSEOG)

Students who have exceptional need may be considered for the Federal Supplemental Educational Opportunity Grant (FSEOG). You can receive between $100 and $4,000 a year, depending on a variety of factors—including your EFC and other aid you may receive.

Individual schools administer the FSEOG, but not all schools participate. The government gives the school a certain amount of FSEOG funds, and then the school is responsible for giving that money out to eligible students. Once the money is gone, the school cannot distribute any additional FSEOG grants that year. So, this is a situation where applying as early as possible is definitely to your advantage, as these grants are given out on a first-come, first-served basis.

TEACH GRANTS

Teacher Education Assistance for College and Higher Education (TEACH) Grants are somewhat unique in that they have some strings attached. TEACH Grants are for students who plan to become teachers—specifically, in a high-need field in a low-income area. You can get a TEACH Grant of up to $4,000 a year.

In order to receive a TEACH Grant, you must sign a TEACH Grant Agreement to Serve. This is a contract in which you agree to teach for at least four years in a high-need field, at a school or educational service agency that serves students from low-income families.

If you do not meet that obligation, the amount you received as a TEACH Grant will be considered a loan, and you will need to pay that money back. This could get costly, as interest will be charged on that amount from the date the grant (now a loan) was disbursed.

SCHOLARSHIPS

Like grants, scholarships do not need to be repaid. However, there usually are some criteria you must meet in order to qualify.

There are many available scholarships out there. Colleges give numerous scholarships, but there are a good number of other sources of scholarship money. Service clubs, companies, and charities give out about $2 billion in private scholarships each year, according to FastWeb, a large scholarship-search provider. Approximately 1 million students receive scholarship money annually, FastWeb says—meaning 1 out of 13 students wins a scholarship.

There are a few common reasons why students don't pursue scholarships:

- **The odds seem impossible.** For the huge, big-dollar scholarships, the competition is intense. This doesn't mean you shouldn't apply, but the odds will be tough. Search strategy: It can be smart to focus on smaller scholarships where the applicant pool isn't so huge. Your chances are often a lot better—and a few small scholarships can add up.
- **They think they won't quality.** True, if you are a genius with perfect SAT scores, your scholarship options are probably high. But there are plenty of scholarships that don't require you to be a child prodigy. Search strategy: Scholarships are available for a wide range of candidates and criteria. Be sure

41

your parents are on the lookout, too. Scholarships may be available through their workplace, professional organizations, or other sources. Give some serious thought as to anything that may help you qualify for a particular kind of scholarship—and think specific and unusual. The narrower the criteria for the scholarship, the fewer applicants there are likely to be.

- **They think the application process will be a hassle.** The application process varies greatly from one scholarship to another. Some require you to submit things, such as a video, an essay, a sample of artwork, or other application materials. However, many simply require an application and a short essay. Search strategy: Look for scholarships where you can complete the application process within a few hours; this seems like a worthwhile investment, considering the potential benefit.

HOW TO FIND SCHOLARSHIPS

Thanks to the Internet, it's easier than ever to find out about scholarship opportunities. Don't get lured in by scholarship search scams that want to charge you money to connect you with scholarships—it's very easy for you to find this *free* information on your own.

There are several large websites and databases, such as FastWeb and Finaid.org where you can search for scholarships. Be sure to enter as much information about yourself as possible. There are many scholarships that are awarded based on certain criteria. These can relate to your family, background, interests, organizations to which you may belong, and other factors.

SCHOLARSHIP APPLICATION TIPS

Here are some scholarship application tips from Scholarship America, a private scholarship and education support organization. Since 1958, Scholarship America has distributed $3 billion in scholarship assistance to 2 million students, funding both entry-level and multiyear scholarships and emergency financial grants. More information is available at www.scholarshipamerica.org.

1. BE PREPARED.

Brainstorm a list of qualifications.

Begin researching scholarships early.

42

2. BE COMPLETE.

Report test scores accurately.

Follow instructions completely.

3. BE CAREFUL.

Review, proof, and revise applications before sending.

Have someone else check your work.

4. BE ON TIME

Meet the deadlines!

5. VISIT THE SCHOLARSHIP COACH.

Visit usnews.com/blogs/the-scholarship-coach for more tips and scholarship info.

MILITARY AID

The government has several programs to provide financial aid for members of the military, veterans, and their family members.

ROTC Scholarships: These are scholarships for military officers in training. You receive scholarship money while attending college in exchange for agreeing to serve in the military for a certain period after you graduate.

Department of Veterans Affairs Education Benefits: The VA administers these programs, which provide educational assistance to veterans, their widows, and dependents. The programs for which you may be eligible will depend on the type, length, and period of military service. There are also special programs to provide benefits to the dependents of military service members who died or became disabled as a result of their service.

For information about education assistance for military families, visit the Department of Veterans Affairs website: http://www.gibill.va.gov/.

STUDENT LOANS

Many students need to take out loans to help cover the cost of their college tuition and other educational expenses. Unlike some other forms of aid, loans must be repaid. So you should always explore any other forms of financial aid that might be available before you consider applying for a loan.

DIRECT LOANS

Federal loans usually offer better interest rates than those offered by private lenders. In addition, the government offers a variety of repayment options (including income-based repayment plans), while private lenders usually have very limited payment plan options.

The largest federal student loan program is the Direct Loan program (officially known as the William D. Ford Federal Direct Loan program). In this program, the "lender" who provides your loan is the U.S. Department of Education.

There are four types of loans under the umbrella of the Direct Loan program:

1. Direct Subsidized Loan: These loans are for undergraduate students with financial need.

2. Direct Unsubsidized Loan: This type of loan is for undergraduate, graduate, and professional students who are not required to demonstrate financial need.

3. **Direct PLUS Loan:** These loans are for undergraduate and graduate students, as well as parents of dependent undergraduate students. These loans help cover the gap in paying for costs that are not met by other financial aid. (The U.S. Department of Education will perform a basic credit check to approve you for a PLUS loan.)

4. **Direct Consolidation Loan:** This type of loan combines all of your existing federal student loans into one comprehensive loan.

SUBSIDIZED VS. UNSUBSIDIZED LOANS

As previously mentioned, some federal loans are subsidized or unsubsidized.

Subsidized loans have to do with financial need. The interest on these loans doesn't accrue while the borrower is in school or in a period of deferment. Interest is also subsidized during the first three years of certain income-based repayment plans. (The name comes from the fact that the government subsidizes the interest on your loan during these periods.) For **unsubsidized loans**, financial need isn't considered. Interest accrues starting from the time the school disburses the loan funds.

PERKINS LOANS

The Federal Perkins Loan Program is another government-backed loan program, but the school awards and manages the loan funds. Students with exceptional financial need receive these loans. With a Perkins Loan, the school is your lender.

HOW MUCH CAN YOU BORROW IN FEDERAL LOANS?

The amount you can borrow in federal loans depends on several factors, including the year in which you are in school. (As you progress into upper levels, the loan limits for Direct Loans increase.)

The following table shows the current loan limits (for the 2013–14 school year), as dictated by the U.S. Department of Education.

UNDERGRADUATE STUDENT	GRADUATE STUDENT
Direct Loans: $5,500 to $12,500 (This will probably include a combination of subsidized and unsubsidized loans.)	**Direct Loans:** Up to $20,500 per year in unsubsidized loans
Perkins Loans: Up to $5,500 per year	**Perkins Loans:** Up to $8,000 per year
PLUS Loans: If you are a dependent student, your parents can apply. They can borrow up to the amount of your college costs that are not met by other sources of aid.	**PLUS Loans:** You can borrow up to the amount of your graduate program costs that are not covered by other sources of aid.

Often, your school will offer you loans for the maximum amount for which you are eligible. You are not obligated to accept this amount (or any of it, actually). If you don't absolutely need it for school, you should decline this money. Remember, this isn't "free money." You will have to pay it back, with interest. You should only take loans that you really need in order to pay for school.

PRIVATE LOANS

Many banks and other private lenders offer student loans. However, the interest rate probably will be higher than it would be with federal student loans. In addition, private lenders probably won't offer you the variety of repayment options the government will. In addition, a private lender will perform a credit check before approving your loan and may even require a co-signer. This is why you should always use federal loans as your first option and only consider private loans if you still need help paying for school after you've taken the maximum amount of federal loans that are available to you.

STUDENT LOAN CONSOLIDATION

Should You Consolidate Your Student Loans?

Before you consider consolidating your student loans, you should ask yourself a few questions. Does the convenience of a single monthly payment benefit you? If your multiple monthly payments are manageable, and you have a good payment system in place, you may not want to consolidate your student loans.

- **How much are you willing to pay over the long term?** Loan consolidation could potentially increase your repayment term, meaning you will pay more in interest. Like a home mortgage or a car loan, extending the years of repayment increases the total amount you have to repay because you will pay more interest in the long run.

- **How many payments are left on your student loans?** If you're close to paying off your student loans, the slightly lower monthly payment might not be worth the time it takes you to consolidate.

What Are The Benefits of Consolidating Your Student Loans?

You may be eligible to combine your federal education loans into a new loan that offers several advantages, including:

- Easier debt management through one lender, the U.S. Department of Education.
- No minimum or maximum loan amounts or fees.
- Time eligibility for deferments is reset, as if you, the borrower, hadn't yet used any deferment time.
- The loan amounts being consolidated that have interest paid by the federal government (subsidized loans) will still be subsidized after the consolidation is complete.
- Reduced monthly payments.

Are Your Loans Eligible for Direct Consolidation?

Most federal education loans are eligible for consolidation into a Direct Consolidation Loan. To be eligible, you must have more than one Direct Loan or Federal Family Education Loan (FFEL) Program loan, or a combination of loans from the two programs. (Note that FFEL loans are no longer being made; all federal loans are now made under the Direct Loan program.) At least one of those loans must be in a grace period, be in deferment, have defaulted, or have payments due (in repayment). If you are in school and have not entered "repayment," (the time when payments are due on your loan), your loans can't be included in a Direct Consolidation Loan (except for loan applications that were received between July 1, 2010, and June 30, 2011).

You may also be eligible if you:

- Include at least one FFEL Loan and have been unable to obtain a Federal Consolidation Loan
- Have been unable to obtain a Federal Consolidation Loan with Income-Sensitive Repayment Plan terms acceptable to you
- Intend to apply for loan forgiveness under the Public Service Loan Forgiveness Program
- Have not been able to obtain a no-interest accrual benefit for active duty

You can consolidate most defaulted education loans if you make satisfactory repayment arrangements with your current loan servicer or you agree to repay your new Direct Consolidation Loan under the Income-Contingent or Income-Based Repayment Plan.

Note: If you have only one Direct Consolidation Loan, you can't consolidate again unless you include an additional loan.

A few types of loans are ineligible for Direct Consolidation. These loans include the following:

- Loans made by a state or private lender that are not guaranteed by the federal government
- Primary Care Loans
- Law Access Loans
- Medical Assist Loans
- PLATO Loans

How Long Will It Take to Consolidate Your Loans?

The consolidation process usually takes between 60 and 90 business days. Applying online can potentially reduce the amount of time it takes to consolidate your loans.

How to Apply

To apply for Direct Loan Consolidation, go online to LoanConsolidation.ed.gov. If all of your student loans are Direct Loans, you can apply over the phone by calling 800-557-7392 (toll-free).

Tips on Paying for College

Make payments while in school: Making payments while in school keeps borrowing costs lower and makes repayment easier. Most, if not all, lenders allow this option with small monthly payments during school.

Shop around: Private loans should be your last stop when looking for financing options. Free money, such as scholarships and grants, and savings should be tapped first followed by federal loans. Researching different loan options can help you find lower interest rates, especially if you have good personal credit.

Take advantage of free money: Every year, hundreds of scholarships and thousands of free tuition dollars are available to students. The good news is many of these scholarships are available year-round, so students shouldn't limit their search to the start of the school year. For example, signing up for and using the scholarship search available on CollegeAnswer.com can give a student access to more than 3 million scholarships.

REPAYING YOUR STUDENT LOANS

When repaying your student loan, consider which repayment plan could best meet your needs. Choosing the right one for your situation is important when keeping your finances in order. Contact the loan servicer (customer service provider) for your student loans to find the best option for you. You can find out which company is servicing your loan by visiting http://www.nslds.ed.gov/nslds_SA/.

STANDARD REPAYMENT

Direct & FFELP Loans:

- Fixed monthly payment until your loan is paid in full (up to 10 years).
- Monthly payments are at least $50.
- Loan is repaid in the shortest amount of time.
- Least amount of interest is paid.

GRADUATED REPAYMENT

Direct & FFELP Loans:

- Payments start low and increase every two years (for up to 10 years).
- This plan works well if you expect your income to increase steadily over time.
- Amount due each month must cover the interest.
- No single payment will be more than three times greater than any other payment.

EXTENDED REPAYMENT

Direct & FFELP Loans:

- Fixed annual or graduated repayment (up to 25 years).
- Must have a total amount of FFELP loans exceeding $30,000 or a total amount of Direct Loans exceeding $30,000 (the $30,000 minimum cannot be a combination of both loan types); Extended Repayment would then apply based on the eligible loan program—for example, if you have $30,000 in Direct Loans and another $5,000 in FFELP loans, Extended Repayment would only apply to the eligible Direct Loans.
- More interest is paid due to the longer loan term.
- All loans must have been disbursed on or after October 7, 1998.

50

INCOME-CONTINGENT REPAYMENT (ICR)

Direct Loans Only:

- Payments are based on family size, adjusted gross income, and total balance of all Direct Loans.

- Payments are adjusted annually.

- Any unpaid interest (due to payment amount) is capitalized annually.

- If you haven't paid your loan in full after 25 years of qualifying payments, the remaining balance will be forgiven.

- You may have to pay income tax on any amount that is forgiven.

INCOME-BASED REPAYMENT (IBR)

Direct & FFELP Loans:

- Your monthly payment will be no more than 15 percent of your discretionary income[1].

- To be eligible, you must have a Partial Financial Hardship[2]—which is based on your total loan debt, adjusted gross income, and family size.

- Your monthly payments will be lower than they would be under the 10-year standard plan.

- Your payments will change as your income and family size change.

- If you haven't paid your loan in full after 25 years of qualifying payments, the remaining balance will be forgiven.

- You may have to pay income tax on any amount that is forgiven.

PAY AS YOU EARN REPAYMENT

Direct Loans Only:

- You must not have had an outstanding loan balance on a Direct or FFELP loan as of October 1, 2007, or no outstanding balance on a Direct or FFELP loan when you received a new loan on or after October 1, 2007.

- You must have received a disbursement of a new Direct Loan on or after October 1, 2011.

- Your monthly payment will be no more than 10 percent of your discretionary income.

[1]**Discretionary income** is your income minus 150% of the poverty guidelines for your family size.
[2]You have a **Partial Financial Hardship** if the monthly amount you would be required to pay on your Income-Based Repayment Plan (IBR) or Pay As You Earn eligible loans under a Standard Repayment Plan with a 10-year repayment period is higher than the monthly amount you would be required to repay under IBR or Pay As You Earn.

- To be eligible, you must have a Partial Financial Hardship—which is based on your total loan debt, adjusted gross income, and family size.
- Your payments will change as your income and family size change.
- If you haven't paid your loan in full after 20 years of qualifying payments, the remaining balance will be forgiven.
- You may have to pay income tax on any amount that is forgiven.

The following chart will give you an idea of how the different repayment plans work.

Consider the total interest accrued and the total amount paid under each option when choosing a repayment plan. All dollar amounts and repayment terms are estimates.

Example 1: Loan balance = $20,000; interest rate = 6.8%

	Standard	Graduated	Extended	Income-Contingent[1] (Direct Loans only)	Income-Based[2]	Pay As You Earn[3] (Direct Loans only)
Monthly Payment	$230	Years 1–2: $158 Years 3–4: $192	N/A	Initial payment: $157 Maximum payment: $182	$166	$110
Term	10 years	10 years	N/A	16 years	17 years	20 years
Total Interest	$7,619	$9,111	N/A	$13,927	$13,725	$26,490
Total Paid	$27,619	$29,111	$7,619	$33,927	$33,725	$26,490

Example 2: Loan balance = $50,000; interest rate = 6.8%

	Standard	Graduated	Extended	Income-Contingent[1] (Direct Loans only)	Income-Based[2]	Pay As You Earn[3] (Direct Loans only)
Monthly Payment	$575	Years 1–2: $395 Years 3–4: $480	$347	Initial payment: $314 Maximum payment: $465	Minimum: $166 Maximum: N/A	$110
Term	10 years	10 years	25 years	18 years	25 years	20 years
Total Interest	$19,048	$22,777	$54,112	$40,215	$49,800	$26,490
Total Paid	$69,048	$72,777	$104,112	$90,215	$49,800	$26,490

Example 3: Loan balance = $100,000; interest rate = 6.8%

	Standard	Graduated	Extended	Income-Contingent[1] (Direct Loans only)	Income-Based[2]	Pay As You Earn[3] (Direct Loans only)
Monthly Payment	$1,151	Years 1–2: $395 Years 3–4: $480	$694	Initial payment: $314 Maximum payment: $988	Minimum: $170 Maximum: $N/A	$110
Term	10 years	10 years	25 years	25 years	25 years	20 years
Total Interest	$38,096	$45,555	$108,222	$171,628	$49,800	$26,490
Total Paid	$138,096	$145,555	$208,222	$196,465	$49,800	$26,490

[1] The ICR plan example is calculated based on an annual gross income of $30,000, not married, and a family size of one living in the contiguous United States. This repayment amount will be recalculated annually and is subject to change based on the poverty guidelines per family size as determined by the U.S. Department of Health and Human Services. This plan has a maximum term of 25 years and is only offered to Direct Loan student borrowers. [2] The IBR plan example is calculated based on an annual gross income of $30,000, not married, and a family size of one living in the contiguous United States. Monthly payment amounts under the IBR plan may change annually based upon the borrower's annual gross income and family size. Any remaining balance, including interest, is forgiven after 25 years of qualifying payments under this plan. [3] The Pay As You Earn plan example is calculated based on an annual salary of $30,000 and a family size of one living in the contiguous United States. Monthly payment amounts under the Pay As You Earn plan may change annually based upon the borrower's annual gross income and family size. Any remaining balance, including interest, is forgiven after 20 years of qualifying payments under this plan.

How to Avoid Delinquency and Default on Your Student Loans

What is delinquency?

Your student loan status will become delinquent if your monthly payment is not received by the due date.

What is default?

If your loan becomes 270 days past due, you are legally in default on your student loan. Default is very serious, and the consequences can harm your credit and hinder your ability to borrow money for future purchases like a car or house.

What are the Consequences of Delinquency or Default?

Delinquency and default are serious. Consequences for having an account status in delinquency or default are the following:

- The entire amount of your loan, including accrued interest and late fees, will become immediately due and payable unless payments are legally postponed with a deferment or forbearance; consult the customer service provider for your student loans (your servicer) for available options.

- Your default will be reported to all national credit bureaus.

- Legal action can be taken against you, and you could be responsible for all attorney fees and court costs.

- A collection agency can be hired to collect the loan balance.

- You will be responsible for paying collection costs.

- Your wages can be withheld (garnished) to pay the loan balance.

- Your federal and state tax refunds can be withheld to pay the loan balance.

- You will not be eligible for any other federal financial aid.

- If your profession requires a license to practice, you can be denied renewal of your professional license until you have made satisfactory arrangements to repay your loan.

Communicating with your servicer is the key to avoiding delinquency and default. Many options are available that can lower or postpone your student loan payments. Stay in touch with your loan servicer. Let them know if you've changed your contact information, and make sure that they know when you've completed your educational program or transferred to another school.

If you find yourself falling behind on your student loans in the form of delinquency or default, consider applying for a deferment or forbearance until you can properly resume payments.

DEFERMENT

A deferment is a period when payment on the principal of a loan is postponed. For subsidized Direct loans and all or a portion of a subsidized consolidation loan, interest payments are made by the federal government.

After the grace period—the six months after graduating or dropping below half-time student status—has expired, borrowers are entitled to a deferment if they meet regulatory requirements. You should continue making payments on your loan until you're notified the deferment is approved.

ELIGIBILITY FOR A DEFERMENT

Your eligibility for a deferment depends on when the loan was made and the individual deferment's requirements.

Eligibility for a deferment does not mean you are required to take it—you may choose to continue making payments on your student loan. Any unpaid interest on unsubsidized loans will be capitalized (added to the principal balance) at the end of the deferment period, increasing the total balance and your monthly payments.

The most common types of deferments are the following:

- School deferment
- Unemployment deferment

- Economic hardship deferment

- Education-related deferment

- Service-related deferment

- Other deferments, which include Temporary Total Disability, Parental Leave, and Public Service

FORBEARANCE

A borrower who is willing but unable to make payments, and does not meet the qualifications for a deferment, may request forbearance. Forbearance allows you to temporarily postpone your payment for a specified period of time. The forbearance will eliminate any delinquency that currently exists on the account, but it won't reverse any derogatory credit information previously reported.

No fees are assessed for obtaining forbearance; however, interest will continue to accrue on your loan(s) during the forbearance period. Interest payments may be made at any time during this time. Any unpaid interest at the end of the forbearance period will be capitalized (added to the principal balance). Capitalization of interest will increase the amount that must be repaid and may result in an increased monthly payment amount.

The most common types of forbearances include the following:

- Hardship

- Reduced Payment

- Internship/Residency

- Student Loan Debt Burden

- Department of Defense (DOD) Loan Repayment Program

- Corporation for National and Community Service (CNCS) Loan Repayment Program/Hardship

IMPORTANT THINGS TO REMEMBER

- Figuring out exactly how much college will cost may take some time and effort—but it may provide some unexpected and interesting results.

- 529 Savings Plans are a great way for you, your parents, and other relatives to help you save money for college.

- There are a number of financial aid options that may be available to you, including scholarships, grants, and student loans.

- There are forms such as the FAFSA and CSS PROFILE® that you may need to complete in order to receive financial aid. Be sure to start working on these forms early, and submit them before the deadlines.

- Student loans can help you pay for school, but they are a debt that you must repay with interest. You should carefully consider any other options you may have before taking out loans, and then you should only borrow the amount you absolutely need to pay for college.

CHAPTER FOUR: CREDIT

Years ago, many people survived without using credit at all (except maybe for a mortgage). These days, trying to live on a cash-only basis is challenging, if not nearly impossible. You need a credit card to rent a car or get a hotel room, and paying bills online, which is easier with a credit card, is becoming more common.

Even if you don't think you'll need credit anytime soon, you need to start getting it now; it takes a while to actually establish a good credit record. Plus, you want to have sufficient credit available and ready to use in case of an emergency, so you don't have to rush to try to get it during a crisis.

Credit comes in a variety of forms: car loans, mortgages, credit cards, personal loans, lines of credit, and more.

CREDIT BASICS

Credit: Credit is your ability to buy something even though you don't have enough money on hand to pay for it, or you choose not to use the money you have on hand to pay for it. When you are approved for a loan or open a credit account, you are allowed to make purchases. You must repay this debt, usually with interest. Sometimes, especially if the debt is for a high amount, the lender will require collateral, which is property that the lender can take if you don't pay back the loan. For a mortgage, that would be the house, and for a car loan, it would be the vehicle. This is secured debt because the lenders have some security to ensure that they will get their money back. Secured loans often offer a lower interest rate than unsecured loans, because with a secured loan the lender has some recourse for recouping their money if you do not repay the debt.

Installment loan: An installment loan is where you borrow a specific amount and agree to make regular payments for a certain period until you have satisfied the loan. Mortgages and car loans are the most common types of installment loans.

Revolving credit: A revolving account means you have a certain amount of credit available, and you can continue to use and repay that credit for as long as you like—assuming your account remains in good standing.

It's not enough just to have credit—you want to have good credit. That means you have a good history of handling credit responsibly and paying your bills on time. Good credit makes you an attractive candidate for a loan, so you will get the best interest rates and terms. On the other hand, if you have bad credit, you are considered a higher risk. As such, you may have trouble getting a loan, and, if you do get a loan, you will probably need to pay a higher interest rate.

TIP

Interest rates can add up quickly. For example, let's say you buy a camera for $350 on a credit card that charges 19 percent interest, and you pay just the $15 minimum on your bill. At that rate, it will take you 30 months to pay it off, and that camera will end up costing you $440 when you add in the interest payments.

Source: Credit Karma

CONTRACT FOR CREDIT

When you request a loan, the lender is required to provide you with a written document outlining the terms of the agreement, including the amount you are borrowing, the amount and due dates of payments, the interest rate and total finance charges you will pay, and any penalties you will incur for late payments.

GETTING A LOAN

We described the basics of establishing a financial identity and getting credit in Chapter Two. The most common types of loans are student loans, car loans, and mortgages. You can also get a personal loan for a variety of reasons (including just to get caught up on bills during a financial crisis), but this may be more difficult to obtain if you have little or no credit history.

INTEREST

Once you have credit, you will become very familiar with the concept of interest—this is the price you pay for using credit. Remember, if you pay your balance in full by the due date, you can avoid incurring interest charges!

Interest charges can really add up if you carry a balance on your credit accounts. This is why it is to your advantage to pay off your card balances. If you cannot afford to pay off your entire balance, pay as much as you can to minimize your balance, and, as a result, the amount of interest the lender will charge you. If you only pay the minimum payment every month, it will take you quite a while to pay off your balance, and you will rack up considerable interest charges.

There are two types of interest rates:

- **Variable:** This is a percentage rate that may change over time, either based on the current prime lending rate or according to the terms spelled out in your contract with the lender.
- **Fixed:** This is a percentage rate that does not change.

YOUR CREDIT REPORT AND SCORE

Your credit history is summed up in your credit report. This is a document that contains all of your major credit-related information, including active accounts, payment history, collection or legal actions, available credit, and other information.

CREDIT BUREAUS

Credit bureaus (also known as credit reporting agencies) play a very important role in your credit situation, even though they don't provide loans or otherwise give credit at all. These agencies gather up all of the information about your financial activities and then provide that information (for a fee) to lenders, credit card companies, auto finance companies, employers, landlords, or others who request it.

There are three major national credit reporting agencies: Equifax, Experian, and TransUnion. Each of their reports may be slightly different, so you should check your report at each agency.

61

Equifax

Phone: 800-685-1111 (toll-free)

www.equifax.com

Experian

Phone: 888-397-3742 (toll-free)

www.experian.com

TransUnion

Phone: 877-322-8228 (toll-free)

www.transunion.com

Each month, creditors update their records and share your account status with the credit reporting companies. The credit reporting companies then update their records and add the current month to the history of how you have paid that account.

EXPERT INFORMATION

"A credit reporting company's role is comparable to a library. A library does not write the books, it just stores them and checks them out. Similarly, a credit reporting company doesn't create the account history, it just stores the history reported by creditors and checks it out to potential new creditors in the form of a credit report. To 'check out' a credit report, a company must meet the membership requirements of the credit reporting company and must have a permissible purpose for getting the report."

Maxine Sweet, Vice President of Experian North America's Public Education Organization

WHAT'S IN YOUR CREDIT REPORT?

A consumer credit report contains four types of information:

1. **Identifying information:** Your name, current and previous addresses, Social Security number, date of birth, and possibly your spouse's name

2. **Account information:** Specific information about each of your accounts, including the dates you opened each of the accounts, the credit limit or loan balance, monthly payment, payment status, and payment history. The listing will also say if anyone else is responsible for the account (for example, if it's a joint account). For open accounts, positive information can remain on your report indefinitely. Most negative information remains for up to seven years.

3. **Public records:** Bankruptcy filings, tax liens, and monetary judgments—the length of time these entries remain on your record varies by the type of record.

4. **Inquiries:** This lists those who have viewed your credit report. Some inquiries—such as those initiated by you when requesting a copy of your own report, or those conducted in relation to employment—are visible only to you and won't be provided to anyone else.

Source: Experian

You are entitled to receive a free copy of your credit report once every twelve months from each of the three credit reporting agencies. You can request your free credit reports at AnnualCreditReport.com (https://www.annualcreditreport.com).

The free credit report you receive will not contain your actual credit score, although you can order that for a fee.

In addition, you are also entitled to a free copy of your credit report from a particular credit bureau if you have been denied credit within the previous sixty days based on information contained in that report.

Watch out for "free credit report" services that actually want to charge you for various services such as credit monitoring.

You can see a sample credit report at http://www.experian.com/assistance/sample-credit-report.html.

When you obtain a copy of your credit report, it will also show you a list of any recent inquiries—meaning, anyone who has requested credit information about you recently.

YOUR CREDIT SCORE

Rather than reading through your entire credit report, there is an easier way for a bank or business to quickly evaluate your credit standing—looking at your credit score, also known as your FICO score.

Credit scores can range between 300 and 850. Obviously, your goal is to get your score as high on that scale as possible.

Your credit score is determined by five factors, some of which are considered more important and therefore are weighted more heavily:

1. **Payment history (35 percent):** Have you paid your bills on time? Have any of your accounts been late? If so, for how long?

2. **Amount owed and credit utilization (30 percent):** What is your total debt? How much of your available credit are you using? (In other words, are your cards maxed out?)

3. **Length of credit history (15 percent):** How long have you had your accounts? Lenders like to see a long record of good payment habits, so the longer your history, the better.

4. **New credit (10 percent):** How many times have you requested credit or opened new accounts recently? Taking out too much credit at the same time might make lenders question whether you will be able to pay all that debt back.

5. **Type of credit (10 percent):** It's good to have a mix of credit types: credit cards issued by a bank, department store credit cards, home equity lines of credit, installments loans, and so on.

> # TIP
>
> Recent grads can open a credit card under their own name to begin building credit. The key is to start small, pay on time, keep your total charges within your credit limit, and pay in full every month—or at least the minimum payment. Choose a credit card that rewards you with every purchase and does not carry an annual fee, such as the new Discover card that offers 1 percent on all purchases and 5 percent on quarterly rotating categories.
>
> Source: Discover.

HOW TO IMPROVE YOUR CREDIT SCORE

There is no magic trick to improve your credit score overnight. The only real way to have a good credit score—and a good report overall—is to pay your bills on time and manage your credit responsibly.

However, there are strategies that can have a relatively quick positive impact on your credit score. (The extent to which these will affect your credit score will depend on several factors, including what your score is and any other credit issues.) Here are some ways to improve your credit score:

- **Open a credit account—and use it sparingly.** If you don't already have credit cards, open one account (even if it's a low-limit account). Then—and this is the important part—use it sparingly. You might think it is best not to use it at all, but that can actually backfire because the account will then be viewed as inactive (and could even be closed due to inactivity). Also, a dormant account doesn't do anything to help show you can pay your bills and manage your credit well. But you don't want to go to the other extreme and max the card to its limit. Instead, use it for small transactions on a regular basis, and then immediately pay off those balances.

- **Obtain a copy of your credit report—and study it carefully.** Many credit reports contain inaccurate items. If you spot any mistakes, getting them removed from your report can help your score.

- **Pay down your balances as much as possible.** Your credit score is affected by your "utilization ratio," which means the level of your available credit that you've actually used. The higher your balances, the less available credit you have. By paying as much of the balances as you can—and then keeping the balances low—you improve your utilization ratio, which in turn helps your credit score.

EXPERT ADVICE

"Your credit report and scores are a reflection of your ability to pay back debts. The scoring models reward consistency and longevity of payments, as well as minimal debt used in relation to amount available to be spent. Your credit report and scores do not take into consideration items such as rent, utility, or cell phone payments. These are accounts that are paid monthly; however, they do not reflect the use of credit, which means the extension of debt. Per-month services are just that, services. They are not accounts in which money is borrowed on the promise of repayment. This does not mean these bills cannot or will not appear on a credit report. If a per-month service account defaults and becomes a collection, then, in this case, it will appear on a credit report and thus decrease the credit rating.

If it's not related to borrowing money, why does it appear on a credit report later? The answer: because it represents an obligation that went unpaid. Variety of credit is important as well. As stated above, on-time payments and utilization of available credit is the key. How do you do this? Have one installment loan, such as an auto loan, personal loan, or student loan. And have at least two credit cards with balances under 30 percent of the limit.

With these accounts, you will get on-time payments, longevity (as long as the credit cards stay open), and a healthy utilization ratio (as long as the credit card balances are low). Head off any non-credit accounts going to collections by ensuring all bills are paid on time. Stay on top of medical bills as well as those that tend to appear from time to time.

In a nut shell, pay your bills on time, and use debt sparingly."

Carla Blair-Gamblian, Home Loan Consultant for Veterans United Home Loans

66

5 SURPRISING THINGS THAT MAY NEGATIVELY IMPACT YOUR CREDIT SCORE

(Courtesy of TransUnion)

1. **City fines and parking tickets:** Often, what starts out as a small fine ends up growing quite a bit—especially if you ignore it, and additional fines or court costs are added. Cities and other municipalities can send even small fines to collections, so make sure that you pay up on time, and clear out small amounts so they don't turn into a big deal.

2. **Back taxes:** Whether taxes are owed to the Internal Revenue Service (IRS) or a local municipality, these can result in liens, wage garnishments, or court judgments—all of which can show up on your credit report.

3. **Unsettled accounts:** If you move or change service providers, be sure to confirm with your utility company or other service provider that you have satisfied all remaining balances—and that your account is listed as closed in good standing. Otherwise, you risk having an account that is listed as delinquent or inactive long after you've forgotten about it.

4. **Hard inquiries:** A "hard inquiry" is when a lender or business checks your credit after you've applied for credit with them. Some surprising places that run hard inquiries include utility companies, cell phone providers, and car rental companies. Too many hard inquiries—especially if they happen in a short period of time—can hurt your credit score.

5. **Closed or inactive credit.** Closing an unused or inactive credit card could reflect as less available credit on your credit history, which is usually seen as a negative. Instead, keep unused credit cards open, and use them for small purchases that you pay off immediately.

WHO CHECKS YOUR CREDIT?

You might be surprised to find out who has been checking out your credit report. Obviously, banks and credit card companies look at your credit history when you apply for a loan or credit card. Others who may be checking your credit, as well, include the following:

- Employers
- Insurance companies
- Landlords
- Utility companies
- Debt collectors

Paying your rent on time now can help you establish a good credit history. In 2010, Experian became the first national credit reporting company to report positive rent payment information. Currently, Experian collects payment information from more than 3,000 apartment communities, and the number is constantly growing.

IF YOU SPOT A MISTAKE ON YOUR CREDIT REPORT

It's fairly common for credit reports to contain mistakes for a variety of reasons. Sometimes it is due to confusion if someone else's name, social security number, and/or other information are similar to yours. Or it's possible that the creditor who provided the information to the credit bureau made a mistake. And, of course, there is the possibility that you've been the victim of fraud or identity theft.

Whatever the cause, if you spot inaccurate information on your credit report, you should file a dispute with the credit bureau right away. You can initiate a dispute claim online, by phone, or through the mail. Be sure to provide as much specific information as possible about the item you are disputing. You should also contact the company or creditor that provided the information to the credit bureau.

MOST COMMON CREDIT REPORT ERRORS

- **Incorrect or outdated personal information:** There is a mailing address on the report, but you never lived there. It is probably a mix up from a person with a similar name.

- **Wrong account details:** One of your credit cards has a different credit limit than what appears on your report.

- **Incorrectly attributed accounts:** There is an account showing up on your report that is your parents' account.

- **Fraudulent accounts:** These are accounts for which you never applied.

- **Inaccurate activity:** It says you have a late payment, but you never paid your credit card late.

HOW TO CATCH THE ERRORS

- Take advantage of getting a free copy of your credit report. Each of the three major credit bureaus will give you a free copy of your report once every 12 months.

- Use a service like Credit Karma that will monitor your credit report and alert you if something significant changes.

FIXING CREDIT REPORT ERRORS

- **First find the right person to contact:** Many consumers make the error of writing directly to the credit bureau, when the error is really with the bank or creditor. You should first contact your creditor/lender directly. Or, to be safe, contact the bank or creditor and the credit bureau so that both are kept apprised of the same information. If, however, the bank says it isn't seeing an error, then you should contact the credit bureau.

- **Gather your proof:** Once you find the error, gather all the proof you will need to support your claim.

- **Write a letter:** Send a letter to the credit bureau reporting the error. Include all your personal information so they know who you are, along with the error you want to dispute. Make sure to send it "return receipt requested," so you know the letter was received. See the Federal Trade Commission (FTC) website for a good sample letter.

- **Make copies:** Keep copies of the letter, the documents proving your claims, and the pages on your credit report containing the errors clearly marked. You will have the information if you need to refer back to it.

- **Wait a month before following up:** You should give the credit bureau time to investigate your claim, which could take up to 30 days. Credit bureaus will send a notification of the dispute to the lender who provided them the information. The lender will investigate and let the bureau know the results. If your dispute is valid, the credit bureau is notified, and they, in turn, have to notify the other two credit bureaus.

(*Courtesy of Credit Karma*)

Be very careful about entering into joint accounts (say, for utilities) with roommates or friends. College students are often hit for joint accounts such as electric bills. If a roommate moves out and doesn't pay, the other is stuck with the bill. If your name is on a joint account, it is your debt no matter who received the goods or services.

How Long Do Items Stay on Your Credit Report?

Negative items can remain on your credit report for up to seven years. However, a bankruptcy, tax lien, or judgment may remain on your report for longer than that.

10 Tips for Managing Your Credit Report to Improve Your Score

(*Courtesy of Experian*)

1. **Establish a credit report:** Creditors need financial references, and that is what your credit report provides. The report's content is used to calculate your credit scores.

2. **Always pay on time as agreed:** Late payments will negatively impact your ability to get credit and are the first signs of impending credit problems.

3. **Have a mix of credit, but obtain and use a credit card:** You decide how to use the card and repay the balance, which tells more about how you make credit decisions than other types of loans, such as auto loans or mortgages.

4. **Use caution when deciding to close accounts:** Closing accounts reduces your available credit. That can increase your total balance-to-limit ratio, which is a sign of risk and can negatively impact your credit score.

5. **Apply for credit judiciously:** If your report shows a lot of recent inquiries, it suggests that you may have just opened a number of new accounts that are too new to be listed on your report yet. This could mean that you have additional debt obligations, and it also may mean that you are overextending yourself. This can make creditors or lenders nervous.

6. **Time is the key:** It takes some time for your credit report to be updated, so balances can't be reduced overnight. In addition, creditors not only look at whether your bills are paid but also at how long they have been current and how far in the past negative information appears. It takes time for scores to improve after you have taken control of your credit.

7. **Demonstrate stability:** Lenders may look beyond your financial transactions and ask how long you have had your job, how long you have lived in the same location, and whether you have built other assets over time.

8. **Have a plan:** Know how you are going to repay the debt when you use your credit card or get a loan, and stick to that plan.

9. **Put credit to work for you:** Use credit as a tool to take advantage of low interest rates, convenient shopping, rewards programs, and financial management. When you are in control, credit works for you.

10. **Share your knowledge:** Share what you've learned with your friends and family so that they can avoid pitfalls and mistakes you might have made.

> # TIP
>
> Establishing a new credit file takes time and patience. This isn't something that you can do overnight, and despite what you might think, there are no shortcuts to establishing good credit. Take your time and be patient. Avoid making applications with places that are likely to turn you down the first time. Each time you make a credit application, it results in an inquiry. If potential creditors see numerous inquiries on your file, it could have a negative impact on results of future applications.
>
> The important thing to remember when you are establishing your credit is to be patient and take your time. Make sure that when you do receive credit, whether it's a loan, credit card, or even utility bills, you make payments on time.
>
> Source: Discover.

FRAUD ALERTS

If you suspect you've been the victim of identity theft—or think your personal information may have been compromised—you can ask the credit bureaus to put a "fraud alert" on your credit reports. This helps protect your identity because it requires potential creditors to go through extra steps to confirm your identity if someone claiming to be you tries to obtain credit. The downside, of course, is that you will also have to go through these extra steps when you are legitimately trying to obtain credit.

To enact a fraud alert, just notify one of the credit bureaus, and they will in turn share your request with the other two credit bureaus.

TOP CREDIT MYTHS

Courtesy of Credit Karma

1. **You only have one credit score.** This is the top credit myth. Consumers really have dozens of different scores, depending on which credit scoring model is used. Each of the major credit bureaus has at

least one model, and many have multiple models. The best thing for consumers to do is to have a few benchmarks since they won't know which model their lender is using.

2. **Carrying a credit card balance will increase your scores.** This is incorrect. Lenders look to see if you are paying your bills on time and building a positive credit history. Keeping a balance will only cost you money because you'll be paying interest.

3. **Checking your credit report will hurt your score.** Checking your own credit report does not impact your score. It's important for people to check their report, and they can for free at least three times a year. Each of the three major credit bureaus is required by law to give people a free copy of their credit report once a year.

4. **Your income weighs into your credit score.** An individual's income is not factored into his or her credit score.

5. **Closing credit cards after paying them off will help increase your credit score.** This is not true, and, in fact, it could actually lower your score. Your credit history is an important part of your credit score. So keeping older cards active and in good standing can help you build your score.

6. **You share a credit score with your spouse.** Just because you now share a last name doesn't mean you also share a credit score. Credit reports are your own, but any shared accounts you have with your spouse will show up on both credit reports.

7. **Shopping for the best loan hurts your score.** It is best to shop for deals especially with a large loan, such as a mortgage. Multiple inquiries for mortgage and car loans are counted as one if they happen within 30 to 45 days of each other.

CREDIT REPAIR SCAMS

Beware of companies that claim they can repair your credit for a fee. There is no way they (or anyone else) can magically improve your credit. The only thing they could legitimately do that would improve your credit score is to remove any inaccurate information, which you can easily do yourself for free.

In addition, some credit repair outfits claim they can create an entirely new financial identity for you. Stay far away from anyone who suggests this, as it may involve your submitting fraudulent documents or providing false information, which can land you in serious trouble.

Michael Dolen, Founder and CEO of Credit Card Forum, says it rarely makes sense to pay for help in repairing your credit. He notes, "They charge you money— usually a lot of it—for things you can do yourself. Worse yet, some operate under the guise of being 'nonprofit,' which is not to be confused with reputable nonprofit charities. The reason credit repair clinics often set themselves up as a nonprofit is because it gives them greater freedom in what they can do and the claims they can make. That's because the Federal Credit Repair Organizations Act restricts what for-profit clinics can say and do. Nonprofits are excluded from those rules."

Instead, Dolen encourages consumers to take a do-it-yourself approach to repairing their credit. "The first resource to turn to is the self-help portal setup by the Federal Trade Commission. Nolo.com has many useful articles on the topic too. Lastly, message boards (such as Credit Card Forum) can be a good resource for connecting with other consumers who may be in the same boat as you. You might be able to find someone who has dealt with the same creditor and can share insight on their experience."

DEBT COLLECTORS

If you have trouble paying your bills and fall behind on payments, you may find yourself in the unpleasant position of dealing with debt collectors.

Debt collectors can be very aggressive in trying to pursue collection of a debt. Unscrupulous collectors will sometimes break the rules or engage in unethical or illegal tactics.

A federal law called the Fair Debt Collection Practices Act (http://www.consumer.ftc.gov/articles/0149-debt-collection) sets rules for what debt collectors can and cannot do in their efforts to collect a debt. Among other things, a debt collector cannot do the following:

- Call you before 8 a.m. or after 9 p.m.
- Contact you at work if you've told them not to do so
- Discuss your debt with anyone other than you, your spouse, and your attorney
- Threaten you or use obscenities

The debt collector must also be able to provide verification that you do in fact owe the debt about which they are contacting you.

We'll discuss more about debt collectors in Chapter Nine.

MAINTAINING GOOD CREDIT

Once you have credit, you then need to protect it and maintain it in good standing. In many ways, this is more challenging than getting the credit in the first place.

Maintaining good credit takes organization, self-discipline, and often some self-restraint. Here is some advice from the folks at Discover.

- **Organization:** Make sure to keep track of all due dates, so you pay all of your bills on time.
- **Self-discipline:** Stick to your budget, and maintain responsible spending and debt-management habits.
- **Self-restraint:** Just because you have the credit available doesn't mean you have to use it. Avoid the temptation to max out your credit cards, and limit the number of cards you have.

We all get busy, but missing a monthly payment may harm your credit. An easy way to prevent this is by setting up automatic payments where your account is debited on a monthly basis when payment is due. Currently the Discover card offers a late payment forgiveness feature, so one late payment will not be held against you.

MANAGING CREDIT RESPONSIBLY

Using credit responsibly is important, but to many people it is not necessarily easy. As we mentioned before, it takes discipline and effort. You must keep track of all of your due dates, make sure you keep your balances under the limits (and, ideally, as low as possible), and only charge what you can afford to pay off quickly.

You also want to keep your amount of credit accounts reasonable. You only want to have accounts that you really need and that you can manage without problems. One of the easiest and most common ways to get into credit trouble is having too many accounts and then running up balances on all of them. It is very tempting to use credit that you have available to you, which is why you don't want to open more accounts than you need.

Of course, part of using credit responsibly involves having some self-restraint. Sure, it would be easy (and let's face it, fun) to go on shopping sprees and max out your credit cards. But that fun would be short-lived, because you would then be weighed down by those large credit card bills and would have to figure out how to pay them.

EXPERT ADVICE

"The biggest myth I see is that many students believe you need to carry a balance on your credit card. What's typically reported to the credit bureaus is your balance at end of a billing cycle (when the bill is issued). That means you don't need to carry a balance to build up your credit history. The amount due on the bill will still be reported whether you pay it in full or not. So pay your bill in full and avoid interest! Some card issuers do report balances on a different day of the month (instead of the cycle close date), but even if that's the case, whatever the balance is on that particular day will be reported to the bureaus."
Michael Dolen, Founder and CEO of Credit Card Forum

76

IF YOU HAVE TROUBLE MAKING YOUR PAYMENTS

If you do run into trouble making your payments, do not just ignore the due dates. You will incur late fees and possibly other charges—plus you may damage your credit. Contact your credit card companies to see if they can offer you any options. They may be able to change or extend your due date to one that's more convenient for you, defer a payment, or offer other options that can help keep your account in good standing.

DON'T BE TOO QUICK TO CLOSE YOUR ACCOUNTS!

Think twice before closing any credit accounts you now have. Closing an account may actually hurt your credit score. This is especially true if you've had the account for a while, because your credit score is based in part on your length of credit. In addition, closing that account can negatively impact your balance-to-limit, which also affects your credit score. As long as the account doesn't charge you a high annual fee, there's no harm in keeping the account open, even if you don't use it. (If you are afraid you might be tempted to use the account, you can always destroy the credit card or store it somewhere that is difficult for you to access.)

5 WAYS TO AVOID DEBT IN COLLEGE

By Rachel Cruze, Author of *The Graduate's Survival Guide* and host of "Generation Change" (https://twitter.com/RachelCruze)

Too many students wander through college and don't think about how the financial decisions within those four years will affect the next 40 years of their lives. The best time to take control of your money is right now. Not when you graduate, not next summer, not next year. Now! By applying these five simple tips, you can avoid making costly mistakes that will leave you deep in debt and struggling to make ends meet.

1. **Make a plan.** I know most college students don't want to do a budget, but it only takes a couple of minutes each month. And even more important, it will prevent you from overspending and relying on a credit card. All you have to do is sit down at the beginning of each month and plan out how you're going to spend every dollar during that month. That's all there is to it!

77

2. Get a job. Yes, you heard that right. If you need extra cash for bills or spending money, get a job. Not only will you be making money, but you'll also be building your skills and resume for after college!

3. Just say "no." As a college student, it's easy to spend money you don't have. Dinner with friends, a quick road trip, spring break. But it's those careless decisions that can quickly get you into deep financial trouble. If you have the cash, great! But if going on that road trip means swiping the credit card, say no.

4. Prioritize. What's more important: Paying your electric bill or going shopping? Buying your books or that new video game? When you have a limited amount of money, you have to set priorities. I'm not saying you can't have any fun, but if you want to stay out of debt, you have to choose wisely where to spend your money.

5. Start saving. At some point you're going to have an emergency. And whether it's a flat tire or a necessary trip home, it's going to require money. By saving up cash for an emergency fund, you'll be able to cover these expenses without using a credit card.

IMPORTANT THINGS TO REMEMBER

- Credit plays an important role in your life—and your financial history and current situation may affect major decisions—so you must establish a good credit history.

- Your credit report is a history of your credit management habits, financial accounts, and other details related to how you handle your finances.

- It takes time to establish a credit history and to repair it after you've had issues, so it's never too early to start building your credit.

- Your credit score is affected by a variety of factors, including your payment history and the types of credit accounts you have.

- Maintaining good credit takes organization, discipline, and self-control.

CHAPTER FIVE: CREDIT CARDS

Credit cards have become a staple of life, at least for many Americans. The 2010 "Survey of Consumer Payment Choice" by the Federal Reserve Bank of Boston showed that 78 percent of U.S. consumers have a credit card, and the average credit card holder has 3.5 cards. This means that it's very likely that if you don't already have a credit card now, you probably will have one (or more) in the near future. So it is important that you educate yourself about credit cards and the best ways to use them responsibly.

Many people are in the habit of paying with plastic for many, if not all, of their purchases. The truth is that charge cards can definitely be convenient, and they are certainly safer than carrying around a lot of cash. But again, it's important to use credit cards responsibly, or you could easily get yourself into financial trouble.

In the last few years, college student ownership of credit cards has declined from 42 percent (2010) to 35 percent (2012), according to research from Sallie Mae, a publicly traded U.S. corporation whose operations are originating, servicing, and collecting on student loans, and Ipsos, a global market research company. Freshmen were least likely to use credit, with 21 percent having a card in their name compared to 60 percent of seniors. The research seems to indicate that most college students exercise caution with credit cards: 33 percent of card holders had a zero balance, 42 percent had a balance of $500 or less, and just 24 percent had a balance of more than $500. Nearly one quarter (23 percent) of parents help pay at least a portion of their student's credit card bill.

Source: https://www.salliemae.com/about/news_info/newsreleases/2013/StudentCreditCards.aspx

---

CREDIT CARD BASICS

You probably already have a basic understanding of how a credit card works, but if not, it's fairly simple:

1. You apply for a credit account with a bank, a retailer, or a credit card company. This could be a national lender/company like Wells Fargo or Capital One, a credit card company like Discover or MasterCard®, or a store or business like Macy's or Mobil.

2. After checking your credit and reviewing your application, the company either denies your request or approves you for a certain amount of credit—this is known as your credit limit.

3. You will then receive a credit card, which you can use to make purchases, or, in some cases, take cash advances through an ATM machine.

4. The amount of these purchases is deducted from your available credit. If your transactions reach or exceed your credit limit, you are said to be "maxed out."

5. You will receive a bill once a month for all of your purchases, and you will be informed of the minimum amount you must pay in order to keep your account in good standing. If you pay off your full balance before the due date, you will avoid incurring any interest charge. Otherwise, interest charges and any other applicable fees will be added onto your total.

Remember: Credit cards are not free money. You are essentially borrowing that money from the company that gave you that card. So there are strings attached—mainly, that you will have to pay them a fee in the form of interest for using that money.

Here are some surprising stats from *Time* magazine: "Only 15% of students with credit cards have any idea how much their interest rate is, and fewer than 1 in 10 students know their interest rate, late fee, and over-limit fee amounts."

Source: http://business.time.com/2012/04/12/college-students-are-credit-card-dunces/#ixzz2X99tPKY2

UNDERSTANDING INTEREST

It's impossible to talk about credit cards without also talking about interest, because that's what causes so many individuals' credit balances to increase so quickly and by so much. As we've previously discussed, **interest** is the fee a bank or a credit card company charges you for the privilege of using their money.

Interest charges can quickly add up, especially if you carry a sizable balance on your cards for a while. Even with relatively small balances, you might be surprised at how much interest can accumulate on that amount over an extended period of time.

IMPORTANT TERMS TO KNOW

Here are some important terms you should know with regard to credit card interest:

Annual percentage rate (APR): The amount of interest you will pay on a particular account, expressed as an annual percentage

Fixed rate: An interest rate that remains the same for the duration of your loan or credit period

Grace period: The time during which you can pay your full balance and avoid any interest charges

Promotional or introductory rate: Card companies will often advertise a special introductory rate, which is very low or sometimes even zero, in order to entice people to open up new accounts. Often these companies will make it easy for you to transfer your balance(s) from other cards over to your new account with them. This may sound like a good deal, and it can be if you can pay off that balance quickly. However, pay attention to the fine print. After a certain period of time, that low introductory rate ends, and the interest charge will jump up to the normal rate, at which point you will be hit with interest charges for any balance that remains at that point.

Variable rate: Many credit accounts charge a variable interest rate—one that can change periodically. Variable rates are usually based on the national prime interest rate.

With some credit cards, you may also be charged an annual fee just for having the account. This fee can vary; annual fees of $50 to $100 are common. You will have to pay this fee regardless of how much, or how little, you use the account.

CREDIT CARD COMPANIES AND COLLEGE STUDENTS

You might say that credit card companies and college students have had a rocky relationship. Traditionally, credit card companies loved college students because they tended to like to spend money. Also, the theory among credit companies was that by enlisting young people as customers as early as possible, they would establish what would hopefully be a long-term relationship with that new customer—one that could prove to be very profitable for the credit card companies.

For their part, college students returned the positive feelings, as they generally enjoyed using credit cards.

EXPERT ADVICE

One of the most common mistakes is applying for and receiving too much credit. The credit limit on a card should not exceed 30 percent of your monthly income. (Example: If you are in college and receiving $1,200/month for rent, food, travel, etc., the credit card limit should not exceed $300).
Kimberly Foss, CFP, personal finance expert and president of Empyrion Wealth Management in Roseville, California

However, the trouble came when the bill was due, and the college students found themselves unable to pay. College students often have little or no available money, and thus often have difficulty paying credit card bills, or any other bills, for that matter.

Making the problem worse, many credit card companies were very assertive, some people would even say overly aggressive, in trying to entice students to open accounts.

John Ulzheimer, President of Consumer Education at SmartCredit.com, explains:

"In the past, college campuses and college students specifically were fair game for credit card companies. Credit card companies were notorious for targeting college students with aggressive marketing tactics, making it nearly impossible to walk around a college campus without being solicited to apply for a credit card in exchange for free 'swag.' This swag was usually some type of college-themed marketing freebie used to entice students to apply for a new credit card. To add insult to injury, these credit card offers were insanely easy to qualify for—if you had a pulse and were currently enrolled as a student, there was a pretty good chance you'd qualify. No job? No income? No problem! Predatory credit card marketing practices and college campuses went hand in hand, and students were considered fair game.

Credit card companies are smart. They saw the future potential for college students to become lifelong customers—especially if they could convince you to sign up and become the first credit card in your wallet. After all, you're working hard for that bright and successful future—a future with lots of potential, a future with a great job and an even better paycheck, the perfect customer with which to build a lifelong financial relationship."

In an effort to help protect college students from running into financial problems due to credit cards, the government enacted some new laws a few years ago, although some experts say they don't go far enough.

"The Credit CARD Act of 2009 attempted to curb credit card debt among college students," says Beverly Harzog, credit card expert and author of *Confessions of a Credit Junkie.* "One of the new rules requires that any individual under the age of 21 has to be able to show proof of income. The guidelines about this are a bit unclear. In fact, it's been reported that some college students have listed their student loans as 'income' on credit card applications. This could end very badly for the student if they don't understand how to use credit responsibly. It's tough enough to graduate with student debt. Any student who has student debt plus credit card debt is going to have a difficult time recovering from this financially. It's very important that any student who has gained access to a credit card—by any means—be vigilant about not carrying a balance. Just use the card to build a good credit history."

Maxine Sweet at Experian offers this advice: "The biggest mistake you can make is to confuse credit with debt. Using credit cards does not mean that you should take on debt. If you pay your balance in full each month, you get to use the bank's money for a month, you have buyer protection, and you never pay a penny in finance charges. If you use your card enough to justify the cost, it can also be smart to pay an annual fee to earn rewards such as cash back or frequent flyer points."

CREDIT VS. DEBIT CARDS

Credit and debit cards are very similar in some ways, but they have some important differences. Like a credit card, a debit card can be used to make purchases at stores or online. It is convenient and lets you avoid carrying a lot of cash around. However, here's the important difference: you use a debit card to spend money that you have in an account, usually a checking account. When you make a purchase, that amount will be deducted from your checking account balance. If you don't have enough funds in your account at the time of your attempted purchase, the transaction usually will be declined. Some banks may allow the transaction to go through but will then charge you an overdraft fee or other charges, so be sure to check your bank's policy.

A debit card does not involve the use of credit. You are simply accessing your own funds. So using a debit card will not help you establish or build your credit history.

Another important distinction is that debit cards do not offer the same types of consumer protection features that credit cards do. Also, remember that if someone gets his or her hands on your debit card, or even just your debit card numbers, he or she can use that information to make purchases or even withdraw money from your account. This may leave you unable to access your money—at least until you process a dispute or claim with your bank.

SECURED CARDS

A secured card is a type of credit card in which you deposit funds into an account that serves as a sort of collateral for the account. Your credit limit is usually equal to this deposited amount. For example, if you deposit $300, your credit limit would then be $300. If you fail to make the required payments or keep the account in good standing, the bank can then use some or all of your deposited funds to satisfy your obligations.

People often use secured cards when they are trying to establish credit or are trying to reestablish good credit after having some credit problems. While they can be an effective way to get started or reestablished—a temporary step until you establish a good enough credit history to get a normal credit card—there are some things you need to watch out for. Secured cards sometimes have hefty fees and high interest charges.

If you do use a secured card, be sure you are aware of all fees and charges you may incur. Also, look for a secured card that will transition into a regular credit account after you've maintained it in good standing for a certain period of time.

John Ulzheimer, President of Consumer Education at SmartCredit.com, says, "If you want to avoid leaving college with massive amounts of credit card debt all you have to do is watch your credit card spending, and only spend what you can comfortably afford to pay off in full at the end of each month when the bill arrives. If you follow this one simple rule, credit card debt is a problem you'll never have to worry about."

PREPAID CARDS

A prepaid card is a cross between a credit card and a debit card. Even though prepaid cards are often called "prepaid credit cards," you are not actually using credit. You "load" the card with a certain amount of money, and that's the amount you have available to spend with the card. In that way, it works more like a debit card or gift card, because you can only spend the amount you've funded. Prepaid cards can also function like a credit card in that one of the major credit card companies, such as Visa or MasterCard, provides them, and, therefore, you can use those cards wherever they are accepted, but with some conditions. Some prepaid cards, such as those you buy at a supermarket or chain store, do not have your name printed on them, so certain stores may not accept them. You also will often have trouble using them to make purchases online. However, for an additional fee, you can sometimes order a personalized prepaid card, which you will receive in the mail. Many prepaid cards are reloadable—meaning, you can continuously add more money to increase or replenish your balance.

Andrew Gillen, Vice President at MasterCard, says prepaid cards can be a useful tool to help with budgeting. "Prepaid cards can be a really cost-effective option, especially as bank accounts have gotten more expensive, and they can help you stick to your budget: If you don't have the money on the card, you can't spend it, unlike a credit card. There are a number of great prepaid cards on the market. Study the fees and other details to pick the one that will work best for you. We think the Western Union® MoneyWise™ Prepaid MasterCard® is a great option. It carries FDIC insurance, MasterCard's Zero Liability protection against fraud or loss, and it has no monthly fee."

John Ulzheimer, President of Consumer Education at SmartCredit.com offers the following credit card advice for college students:

"The CARD Act has made great strides in protecting students from predatory credit card practices. Still, young people have to watch out for remaining credit card traps. The most important advice I can give is that you read and fully understand the terms and conditions before you apply for a card. Here are a couple of the most important things to watch out for:

- **Introductory teaser rates.** Don't be fooled by the 0% introductory teaser incentives. These offers can be great deals, but introductory rates are temporary, and you'll want to pay close attention to the ongoing rate after the intro period expires.
- **Annual fees.** Many cards, especially those that offer rewards or cash back incentives, also include annual fees. In many cases, the annual fee is waived the first year, but it will kick in every year thereafter. So it's something to pay attention to, especially when there are a number of other credit cards on the market that don't carry an annual fee. Be aware of all possible credit card fees before you make a selection."

CREDIT CARD SECURITY

As with any other type of financial information, you want to protect your credit card information—and the card itself—and you need to be very careful about how and where you use it. Carefully monitor your credit card account activity; you can do this easily online or from your Smartphone. If you notice anything suspicious or see any unauthorized charges, notify your credit card company immediately.

REWARDS CARDS/PROGRAMS

How would you like to get an exciting bonus simply for following your normal routine? That's the idea behind a rewards card. A rewards card is a credit or loyalty card that lets you earn various types of rewards in return for your usage. The rewards may be in the form of cash, points, discounts, or other incentives.

HOW IT WORKS

You earn rewards by using your card for purchases, so you can get rewarded for buying everything from groceries to gasoline. You can earn rewards for almost everything you pay for with your card, including travel, entertainment, and perhaps even your bills or taxes. Rules vary by card issuer and program.

TYPES OF REWARDS

There are different types of rewards card programs. Cash-back rewards programs, as the name implies, let you earn money by getting cash back—a sort of rebate based on your purchases. With points programs, you earn points, which you can then redeem for merchandise, gift cards, travel, or other items. Airlines miles are one of the most common types of rewards.

You can usually redeem your points quickly and easily online. Some rewards programs have a tiered structure, with several levels of earned points for different types of purchases. The card issuer may also have special promotions where you earn higher bonus points for purchasing from certain businesses or retailers. Along the same lines, you may get a bonus if you redeem your points for gift cards or merchandise from specific retailers.

THE BEST PART

The best part about using a rewards card is that you get rewards for doing things you normally would do anyway. So you may accumulate rewards without even realizing it and without changing any of your normal habits. It's painless and effortless. If you pay your card balance every month to avoid interest payments, the rewards come at no cost to you. Some programs do charge fees, though, so be sure to read all of the fine print.

BANK REWARDS CARDS

Rewards cards offered by banks often provide many additional ways for you to earn points. You may be able to earn rewards for bank-related tasks such as applying for a loan or setting up online banking, direct deposits, or automatic bill payments.

CHOOSING THE RIGHT REWARDS CARD

Rewards cards, and the conditions and polices that go along with them, vary greatly, so it's important to choose your card carefully. A rewards program should complement your lifestyle and spending/banking habits so that it offers you the maximum point-earning opportunities. A single credit card company may have several different types of rewards programs, so compare them, and choose the one that's the best fit for you.

With some banks or credit card companies, you are automatically enrolled in the rewards program if you have a qualifying type of account. Otherwise, you apply for a rewards card in the same way as you would apply for any other type of credit card.

THE MOST IMPORTANT THING TO KEEP IN MIND

If you pay off your card balance in full every month, the rewards you earn are like a free bonus. However, if you use the card to earn points or rewards, but carry a balance from one month to the next, the interest and fees you will incur will likely end up costing you more than any rewards you may have earned.

COMMON CREDIT CARD PITFALLS

Here are a few common mistakes people make with their credit cards:

- **Opening too many accounts at once.** This not only can this hurt your credit score, but it also can be very tempting to splurge and rack up high bills, especially if you haven't had credit before.

- **Paying only the minimum every month.** If you just pay the minimum amount due on your bill, it will take you a long time to pay off the balance, and, meanwhile, you will pay considerable interest charges.

- **Being lured in by low teaser rates or introductory offers.** Many people who open accounts with these teaser rates fail to pay off their balance before the rates reset to the higher normal rate, and thus they incur interest charges that can be quite costly.

EXPERT ADVICE

"While you may want a credit card when you turn 18 for emergencies and to build your credit, it's important to be conscientious about paying off your bill each month on time. Late fees and high interest rates can be a killer on any attempts to maintain a balanced budget when you are starting out. If you do fall into the trap of building some credit card debt, work hard to pay it off as quickly as possible. Don't just pay the minimum required payment—it is the MINIMUM, but it should not be all you pay. Focus on getting this debt paid off before attempting to put aside money in any other savings vehicle."

Mindy Hirt, CFP®, Wealth Advisor at Argent Trust Company

IMPORTANT THINGS TO REMEMBER

- Credit cards can be a valuable financial tool and can help you establish and build credit, but they must be used responsibly.

- If you carry a balance on your credit cards, the interest charges and other fees you will incur can quickly add up and can cause your balance to grow a lot and quickly.

- There are several types of credit cards available. The best choice for you will depend on several factors, including your spending habits and credit history.

- If you have little or no credit history or have had credit issues in the past, a secured card can be an effective way to build or rebuild credit, but it can involve some high fees, so you should only use it for a limited time until you can get a regular credit card.

- Protect your credit card information and the card itself, and be very careful about how and where you use it.

92

Chapter Six:
Jobs and Working

By the time you reach college, you have likely already had at least one job of some sort, even if it was just an informal thing like babysitting or mowing lawns. So you may be somewhat familiar with the idea of doing work in order to earn money. But your college years are often when you get your first "real" job—meaning, a formal situation where you have a work schedule, a boss, co-workers, and an official paycheck.

Even if you've had other formal jobs before, this may be the first time when you need your paycheck in order to pay important bills, as opposed to using it for spending money.

Either way, your earnings at this point are probably more important than ever. So you want to be sure you are as prepared as possible—not only to get the job but also to handle the money you earn wisely.

Your First Job

Your first job can take many forms. It may be a weekend job at the mall, a part-time job near campus, or perhaps even a work-study job or other on-campus position. Depending on your class schedule and financial needs, you may even work a full-time job while in school, although that can be tough to balance while also keeping up with your courses.

Working "Off the Books"

When you do informal jobs like babysitting, mowing lawns, helping people with computer issues, and so on, usually you are not considered an actual employee. You are generally paid cash, you don't get an actual paystub, and you don't have taxes or other deductions taken out of the money you are paid. This type of job is usually referred to as being paid "off the books" or "under the table" because it's not done through a formal process or as part of a typical business accounting system. While you may be excited about the fact that you're earning cash without having to give "Uncle Sam" a cut, there are a few downsides to this type of gig. For one thing, you aren't paying anything into your Social Security fund or other type of long-term plan. And, from a budgeting standpoint, these jobs are usually unpredictable and sporadic—meaning you may not know when or if you will have money coming in. While this might be fine when you are in high school, once you get to college and have more bills to pay, it can be difficult to survive on this type of work because it can make planning your budget a challenge.

Working on the Payroll

For most jobs, you will be employed as part of the official staff. This means you will receive a regular paycheck, which is processed through the employer's accounting or payroll department.

Being paid on the official payroll can have advantages and drawbacks. On the unpleasant side, the company or organization will take taxes and other deductions out of your paycheck. You will also have to deal with a certain amount of paperwork, such as completing tax forms and providing documentation that proves your citizenship status and identity or shows that you are legally allowed to work in this country.

However, the upside is that your official employment status makes you eligible for more protections and benefits under the law, since the government has many rules about how employers can treat workers.

Minimum Wage

For most positions, employers are required to pay you at least minimum wage. There are some exceptions, such as when you work in a restaurant as a server and receive tips. Some exceptions are also allowed for high school students and full-time college students who are employed under certain programs while in school.

As of this writing, the federal minimum wage is $7.25 per hour, but some states have their own minimum wage, which may be higher than that. So depending on where you live, you would get paid at least whatever your state's minimum wage is.

The U.S. Department of Labor's Wage and Hour Division (http://www.wagehour.dol.gov) has information and resources related to minimum wage that may be helpful to you. Their website also contains information about child labor laws, rules regarding young workers, and other job-related regulations.

94

WORK-STUDY JOBS

The Federal Work-Study Program provides part-time jobs to students who need financial assistance. The types of jobs available can range from tutoring to helping out in the dining areas or computer labs at colleges or universities. While most work-study jobs are on campus, sometimes they are off campus at a nonprofit organization or public agency. Your eligibility for a work-study job is determined by financial need—in other words, by your EFC, which is based on the information in your FAFSA. When you complete the FAFSA, be sure to check the box that asks if you are interested in work-study jobs.

Although a work-study award is considered part of your financial aid package, the funds are given differently. Unlike other forms of aid, which are credited toward your tuition bills, with work-study, you receive an actual paycheck. Your hourly rate must be at least minimum wage, but it can be more. The number of hours you can work per week will depend on your work-study award.

Your school must participate in the Federal Work-Study Program in order for you to get a work-study job, so be sure to check with your school's financial aid office to see if it participates.

Schools have a limited number of work-study jobs available, so if you want to secure one, you must start looking as early as possible. Your school's financial aid office will be able to tell you how to find available positions. At some schools, work-study opportunities are listed on the school's website.

The process of applying for a work-study job can vary widely depending on the school and the type of position. Certain positions require you to have already completed a specific number of courses or to be enrolled in a specific major.

Once you do have a work-study position, remember to take it seriously and treat it just as you would any other job. While some work-study positions try to accommodate students' academic workload by allowing them to work on schoolwork during slow periods, you should not assume that you will be able to slack off. In addition, you'll want to show your boss that you are a responsible, hard-working employee so that he or she will give you a good reference when you apply for other jobs in the future.

FINDING A JOB

There are many different ways to find a job, although the best methods may depend on what type of job you're seeking. To increase your odds of finding a job, it's usually best to combine several of these methods, just to make sure you don't miss out on any good opportunities.

CLASSIFIED ADS

For a long time, this was pretty much the only way to find a job. These days, newspapers are shrinking, or going out of print completely, and classified sections are getting very small. While it's still worth taking a few minutes to check them out every day, you probably won't find much. Most likely the ads you do see mainly will be for entry-level jobs in retail, food service, and construction.

TIP

Many newspapers and news sites now post their classified ads on their websites, so it's easy for you to check the ads of several different sites/papers quickly without having to buy any newspapers.

This is the most basic, low-tech method. As you can probably guess, this means you just walk in and fill out an application. Often, the hiring staff will then need to review your information, perhaps check your references, and, if all goes well, someone will eventually contact you for an interview. Sometimes, though, if an employer is badly in need of help, he or she may even interview you right on the spot. The interview may actually consist of a relatively informal chat about your availability and experience.

Walk-in applications are most common with retail stores and, in some cases, factories, although many of these companies are also increasingly using online applications.

ONLINE APPLICATIONS

More and more companies are accepting online applications these days. In fact, at some companies, that's the only way you can apply, as they no longer accept paper applications.

If there are specific companies for which you would like to work, you can go directly to their websites to check out openings and apply online as well as obtain details on how to apply. If you don't have specific companies in mind, you can browse listings from many employers on online job sites, which we will discuss in more detail later in this section.

Make sure you are well-prepared when submitting an online application. Don't be surprised if it takes more time than you expect. Often there are several steps involved and several different documents you must submit. Take your time and read the directions carefully, making sure you complete all steps. Otherwise, your application may be considered incomplete, and it may not even be submitted or accepted.

It will make things easier if you have some basic documents ready in advance. This can also save you a lot of time, as you won't be scrambling to try and locate information, or remember details, as you are trying to complete the application. A lot of online applications use the same basic documents or information—such as a resume, cover letter, and perhaps your work samples, depending on the type of job you are seeking. So if you keep these materials handy—storing them on your computer is probably the best strategy—you will be able to complete online applications much more quickly.

KEYWORDS

When applying for a job online, it's important to think about keywords. These are important words or phrases related to the position and skills involved. Many companies now use an automated system to process/review applications and resumes. The system may be programmed to look for specific keywords. If your information doesn't match, you may not be at the top of the candidate list. In some cases, the system may reject your application completely.

A good way to figure out the best keywords to use is to study the job ad or posting carefully. Look at the desired skills and experience, especially anything that is labeled as critical or required, and use the same terms in your application or resume.

Online Job Sites

A great way to find and apply for many positions at different companies is to use a jobs-search website, such as Indeed, CareerBuilder, or SimplyHired. Most of these sites work like a search engine—they serve as a central location where you can search thousands of listings from many sources. To help you find things quickly, they have lots of criteria that you can use in order to narrow your search. For example, if you only want to look at jobs in your local area, you can specify that geographic location. And of course, you can also search by keywords or job titles. You will then be able to view the original job posting, where you can usually apply online.

LinkedIn

LinkedIn is a great resource for job seekers. It's not just a job site; it's also a major social networking service. Unlike other social networks like Facebook and Twitter, LinkedIn isn't designed to be a place where you share updates about your weekend plans or personal life. Instead, LinkedIn is a professional networking site—that means you use it to make and maintain professional connections, do work-related networking, and, as previously mentioned, find out about job opportunities.

But first, you should create a LinkedIn profile, which is free. This lets people learn more about you, especially your educational background and work history. If you are still in school and have little or no work history, you might feel like you don't need a profile or don't have enough information for one, but you should still create at least a basic profile. This can be useful in helping you establish valuable contacts, because people will usually check out your profile if you reach out to them via LinkedIn. Even if your resume/history is a bit thin, it shows you are making an effort to establish yourself professionally and make some initial networking efforts. Plus, even a short profile can still contain valuable nuggets of information. For example, a prospective contact may discover that you are a student at her or his alma mater, which may make her or him more enthusiastic about connecting with you than someone who attended a different school.

Once you have a LinkedIn profile, you can then search the site's job postings. A great thing about LinkedIn job postings is that a representative of a company often posts the jobs, so you will have an actual contact name if you have any questions. Another helpful aspect is that you can search your network to see if you know anyone at that particular company. You may have to go through a "few degrees of separation," meaning, you may know someone, who in turn knows someone, and so on, to get to an actual company contact, but at least it is a start.

Even if there isn't a specific job opening at the moment, professional contacts can be very helpful. They may be able to provide some valuable tips or inside information about the field or company in which you are interested. Perhaps, they would even agree to do an "informational interview" or serve as a sort of mentor or advisor to you.

TIP

Keep in mind, a large percentage of available jobs are never actually posted publicly anywhere. That's why it's important to make as many contacts in your target industries, or at your dream employer, as possible. They can help alert you to "hidden" opportunities that might not be advertised.

SOCIAL NETWORK RULES FOR JOB-SEEKERS

Be very careful what you post on social networking sites! This is a good rule of thumb in general, but it is especially important when you are looking for a job.

A recent CareerBuilder survey found that at least 20 percent of employers now use social media sites to screen potential job candidates, and that figure is sure to increase as more employers become concerned about the online activities of employees or potential employees.

To keep employers from running the other way, here are some things that shouldn't be visible on your social networking profiles/pages:

- Photos that depict you engaging in illegal or offensive behavior
- Obscene language or gestures
- Negative comments about your current or previous job or employer
- Anything that makes you look like an undesirable employee, such as pictures of you goofing off at work, or comments about how you came to work with a hangover

---

99

Even if you are of legal drinking age, pictures of you partying or hanging out at a bar are probably also not a good idea, because they make employers worry that your social life will be your priority, as opposed to your job.

Remember, privacy filters can be your friend in this situation! If you want to share pictures of your spring break trip or the concert you attended this weekend, make sure they are only visible to your friends. Keep in mind, though, that there's still no guarantee of complete privacy (one of your friends could, in turn, post those pictures on his or her page, for example). When in doubt, play it safe and don't post anything online that you wouldn't want a potential employer to see.

EXPERT ADVICE

"I personally worked four jobs in college, played NCAA D-III basketball for my college, double majored in math and history, and was active in a few social organizations. Having a job not only helped me with my time management, but it provided extra income for me to save and pay off my student loans sooner than later. Most kids get jobs to pay for beer money or extracurricular activities; however, even if they put $50 a month toward their student loans while they're in school, they'll be able to save money in interest over a long period of time."
Cristina Briboneria, CFP®, Vice President and Private CFO at oXYGen Financial, Inc.

SCHOOL RESOURCES

Most likely, your school has some resources that can help with your job search, and not just for on-campus or school-affiliated jobs. Here are some possible resources you may find at your college or university:

- **Career Services:** Most schools have some sort of career office or department, although the services and resources they offer can vary widely. At a bigger school, there may be a large staff of career counselors and job placement specialists who can help you. Online career resources and job search tools or

100

databases are also common. The school may also host job fairs where you can meet with employers who are recruiting new employees. At smaller schools, resources and services may be limited, and this department may consist mainly of some sort of job listing system where employers can post notices about available positions.

- **Alumni Network:** Another valuable resource is your school's alumni network. While this network may not share actual job postings, the group can help you locate valuable contacts at your target companies. When you are making "cold calls"—calling someone that you don't know, out of the blue—establishing that you have something in common is often a good ice-breaker. Most people are eager to help students from their alma mater. If your school doesn't have an online alumni directory, do a search on LinkedIn for people in your field of interest who attended your school.

Dr. Clay Singleton, Professor of Finance at Rollins College's Crummer Graduate School of Business, shares two mistakes that college students commonly make during the job-hunting process:

1. **Underestimating one's job hunting expenses:** "One reason to go to college is to get a good job after graduation. Actually, you need a job before you graduate. To get a job, you have to find one—it will not find you. There is a career center on almost every campus that will help you with your resume and even line up interviews with prospective employers. Even so, it is up to you to convert job interviews into job offers. To get the offer you want, you might need to travel at your own expense. You will certainly need business attire and probably more than one outfit. As a general rule: the bigger the city, the more formal the dress. Most business employees dress in 'business casual,' but it is always better to dress appropriately. You cannot count on buying suitable clothes the day before the interview. Set aside some funds to cover your interview expenses, and plan ahead so when the right job comes along, you will be ready."

2. **Working too much during the school year:** "Most students need a part-time job to help meet expenses. Remember your first priority is to do well in school. While working two or three part-time jobs is tempting, don't spread yourself too thin. Part-time jobs have a way of evolving into full-time jobs, but normally these are not the kind of jobs you want after you graduate. Strive for balance in your work-school-social life. If you find your school work suffering, cut back until you can manage both work and studies. This is simple, commonsense advice, but it is so easy to fall into the trap of letting money drive you."

UNDERSTANDING YOUR PAYCHECK

With your first real job comes your first paycheck—something you've likely been eagerly anticipating. However, the excitement may not last long, once you rip open the envelope (or, in today's world, check your bank balance online) and see your actual pay amount.

That's because there can be a big difference between the amount you earn (your gross pay), and the amount you actually receive (your net pay, also known as your take-home pay). Your employer is required to deduct certain things from your pay. This includes taxes—mostly likely, several different kinds, including federal, state, and local—as well as any required deductions for unemployment compensation and other programs. In addition, your employer may have deducted fees for other expenses, such as for health insurance, parking, or other items.

TIP

You should always review your pay stub carefully as soon as you get it. Make sure you have been paid for the correct number of hours you worked, and watch for any possible errors. Should you spot any mistakes, notify your employer right away.

ANALYZING YOUR PAYCHECK AND RELATED TAX ISSUES

PaycheckCity.com is a website that offers employees self-service tools for paycheck management, including free personal finance calculators. You can check out "what-if" scenarios using your wages and other paycheck figures to determine the impact certain actions would have on your take-home pay.

HELPFUL INFO ABOUT YOUR PAYCHECK

Gross Pay vs. Net Pay

- **Gross Pay:** the total wages you earn for the pay period. This is what you earn before taxes.

- **Net Pay:** the amount of money you actually receive on pay day. This is your take-home pay.

Taxes Taken Out of Your Paycheck— Where Does That Money Go?

- **Federal taxes:** These include FICA (social security,) Medicare, and federal income tax.

- **State taxes:** State income tax varies by state.

- **Local taxes:** Many cities, jurisdictions, and school districts have a local tax.

  Your employer calculates all of these taxes and other deductions based on your gross pay.

How Much Does Your Employer Pay in Taxes to Have You as an Employee?

- **Federal and state tax:** You pay 6.2 percent and 1.45 percent of your gross pay for federal and state tax, respectively. Your employer also pays that amount to have you as a worker.

- **Unemployment insurance:** This is anywhere from 0.5 percent to 10 percent of your salary.

- **Worker's compensation:** Depending on how risky your job is, this can range from 1 percent to 11 percent of your salary.

  There may be other deductions, but these are the most common. When you are negotiating your starting salary or asking for a raise, consider what the cost is to your employer beyond your gross pay. The previous information only includes taxes. Other benefits, such as medical insurance, paid leave, or retirement savings matches, cost your employer even more.

What Is a Federal Form W-4?

- This is a form that determines how much federal income tax your employer needs to withhold from your paycheck. It doesn't determine how much you will owe, just how much will be taken out of your gross pay each payday that will be applied to your income tax liability that is calculated on the annual 1040 form.

- Social Security and Medicare taxes are not calculated using the Form W-4.

- Some states also have W-4 forms.

How to Determine Your Filing Status and Exemptions

- At the federal level, you have a choice of selecting married, single, or head of household.

- For exemptions, use the Form W-4 worksheet to calculate the number of exemptions you should claim.

Why You Don't Want a Tax Refund at the End of the Year and How to Avoid Paying Too Much—or Too Little—in Taxes

- Most tax seasons, about 75 percent of individual taxpayers will receive a federal income tax refund, and the average refund totals approximately $3,000.

- This means that despite how much Americans hate paying taxes, most of us overpay!

- You are better off making that money work for you throughout the year by ensuring you withhold the right amount from each paycheck.

- If you overpaid taxes last year, increase the number of exemptions on your W-4 to withhold less. If you underpaid, decrease the number of exemptions.

If Your Employer Offers a 401(k) or Matches a Percentage of Contributions

- This is essentially free money! Take advantage of it!

- As a young person, it is difficult to imagine retirement, but the money you save early in your career will grow the most by the time you reach retirement.

- If your employer offers a 401(k) match, contribute up to the maximum amount (typically 3 to 6 percent of your gross pay) to ensure you take advantage of the match.

[Note: We will discuss retirement plans in greater detail in Chapter Ten.]

What Are Pay Periods?

Pay periods are how often you get paid. Here are the possible ways:

- **Weekly:** You get paid once a week.
- **Bi-weekly:** You get paid every two weeks. Note that two to three times a year, this pay period results in a three-paycheck month. Your employer pays you 26 times per year.
- **Semi-monthly:** This is a pay schedule that results in your employer paying you on two days of each month, for example, the 1st and the 15th. This means that your employer pays you 24 times per year.
- **Monthly:** Your employer pays you once a month.
- **Yearly:** Your employer pays you once a year. (This is very rare.)

Source: PaycheckCity.com

TYPES OF PAY

There are several different types of pay structures—meaning, the system that determines how much, and possibly how often, you will get paid.

HOURLY

This is probably the most common type of pay structure, especially for entry-level and mid-level positions. An hourly system is pretty easy to understand: you take your hourly rate, multiply it by the hours you worked, and that's your total gross pay. There are times when you may receive more than your normal hourly rate—if you work overtime, for example, or work on a holiday—in which case you would obviously have to adjust the figure you use for this multiplication.

SALARY

A salary-based pay system is more common for managerial jobs and other upper-level positions. This means you receive a set amount per year (or month), regardless of how many hours you work. (However, depending on labor laws that may apply and the type of position, your employer may still be required to pay you overtime if you work more than a certain number of hours in a week or pay period.) People who are paid on a salary structure sometimes get paid once a month, as opposed to the weekly or biweekly pay structure that is typical with hourly employees.

Abby Euler, General Manager of Salary.com, says you shouldn't be afraid to negotiate the initial job offer you may get. "Many students are so grateful for their first full-time position they often don't feel they can negotiate anything before signing a job offer. This is a crucial mistake and can cost students—who may be carrying huge student loan debt—thousands in salary. Keep in mind, you may not be able to negotiate your salary off the bat (remember vacation and flexible work schedules are also negotiable), but you can ask for a six-month performance review to revisit your compensation. All in all, arm yourself with data—use Salary.com to look at comparable salaries in your industry and region to ensure that you enter in at a total compensation package that is competitive and reflects your worth to the company."

Euler adds it is also important to try and find a career you enjoy. "During college, all students seek to find a career that strikes a balance between their passion and getting paid well. You should absolutely understand what the starting salaries are for jobs that interest you but also look at what the long-term earning potential would be as you progress along a chosen career path. Buying your first home, taking vacations, having children, or retiring in Europe may seem far away today, but ensuring that your career will bring lasting financial fulfillment is something you can control now—and that you will thank yourself for doing for many years to come!"

PROJECT-BASED

This type of pay system is usually related to freelance work or other situations where you work on an occasional or irregular basis. In this case, you probably are not considered a staff employee but instead are viewed as a freelancer, consultant, or vendor. The terms and structure of this type of arrangement can vary. You may get paid a flat fee for a certain project—say, $100 for writing a short article—or you may get paid an hourly rate for the amount of time it takes you to complete a project. In the past, companies sometimes would try to avoid paying taxes and other benefits for workers by claiming the workers were freelancers even though the workers were staff employees. However, the IRS has strict rules about how workers are classified, and what determines whether someone is a freelancer or an employee. Lately, they have been cracking down on companies that try to skirt the rules.

COMMISSION

Getting paid on commission means that your pay is based on how much you sell. Lately, the commission structure has expanded to include non-sales positions in which your performance or output is judged, based on some other type of figure(s). For example, some websites pay writers based on the amount of traffic their stories receive. A commission is often based on a percentage of the total dollar amount of your sales.

BONUSES OR INCENTIVE PAYMENTS

If you are lucky, sometimes you will get something extra in your paycheck. This may be in the form of a bonus or incentive payment—perhaps because you met a quota or otherwise performed exceptionally well. Some companies also offer something called profit-sharing, which means all of the employees get extra money at certain intervals if the company does well.

Many companies give you the option of receiving your pay in the form of direct deposit. This means your pay is automatically deposited into your bank account on payday. At some companies, in fact, direct deposit is required, and you don't even have the option of getting a paper check. Direct deposit is very convenient because you don't have to worry about losing your check or bother with the hassle of taking your check to the bank to cash it.

FRINGE BENEFITS

While your pay may be the form of compensation that's most important to you, there are other types of rewards/compensation that you may get as part of your employment. These are called fringe benefits, and they can include things like health insurance, paid time off, tuition reimbursement, education benefits, and more. In higher-level jobs, benefits may include nice perks like a company car, expense account, or company credit card.

While fringe benefits may not put any additional cash in your pocket, they are very important. In particular, health insurance, and related benefits like vision and dental coverage, can be very valuable, because you can save money on doctor bills and medical expenses.

EXPERT ADVICE

"When you get your first job in the career that you want to be in, consider getting supplemental disability insurance (also known as income protection insurance) and life insurance early on. Many people believe they are invincible when they are younger or that they don't need it, but one thing to consider is you can lock in a significantly lower rate as a 21 year old versus a 30 year old."
Cristina Briboneria, CFP®, Vice President and Private CFO at oXYGen Financial, Inc.

WAGE RULES AND REGULATIONS

There are many laws and regulations that relate to various aspects of employment: wages, working conditions, harassment, discrimination, and so on. These are too complicated and numerous to explain in detail here, especially since they can vary by state and city, but you should be able to find out about employment laws that may affect you on your state's Department of Labor website. As we mentioned previously, the U.S. Department of Labor site has a great deal of information about federal employment laws.

JOB-RELATED STATISTICS

Here are some interesting (and perhaps a bit unsettling) job-related statistics, courtesy of American Consumer Credit Counseling:

- Unemployment rate for young college graduates (ages 23–25) in 2011 was 8.8 percent, a slight decrease from 9.1 percent in 2010.

- Of those who wanted to be working full-time, 19.1 percent were working part-time or had given up looking for work.

- 37.8 percent of young graduates had jobs that did not require a college degree (as opposed to 31 percent in 2007).

- Unemployment rate for high school graduates in 2011 was 19.1 percent.

Source: http://www.consumercredit.com/financial-education/student-loans/the-facts.aspx

Still considering your career choice? Check out the following chart of projected job growth:

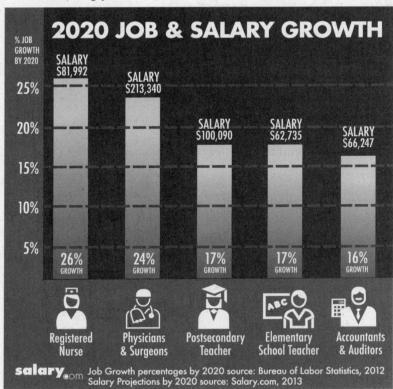

HEALTH INSURANCE TIPS FOR COLLEGE STUDENTS

According to Carrie McLean, Director of Customer Care at eHealthInsurance.com, as part of the health reform law, individuals have from October 2013 through March 31, 2014, to select their health insurance plan for 2014. She notes, "As of that date, most people without employer-based health insurance will be required to purchase coverage on their own." Many colleges and universities already require students to have coverage. But what are the coverage options, and how can you make the most of your health insurance dollars?

Here are a few tips:

Know your options, and don't wait to get coverage. Though college-age young adults are most likely to be uninsured, they may have more coverage options than almost anyone else. For example:

- **Staying on mom and/or dad's plan:** The health reform law now allows parents to keep adult children enrolled in the family health plan until age 26, even if they are not in school or living at home.

- **Getting coverage through an employer:** Many employers offer health insurance coverage; beginning in 2015, all employers with 50 or more workers will be required to offer coverage.

- **Buying your own individual health insurance plan:** This is a good and often affordable option for many young adults, especially if they're going to school outside of the family health plan's coverage area. Just remember that you can still be turned down for pre-existing conditions until 2014. In 2014, you'll be able to buy an individual plan through a state-sponsored marketplace or a licensed agent like eHealthInsurance.com, and you may qualify for subsidies.

- **Enrolling in a school-sponsored plan:** In the past, some of these plans weren't as helpful as they could have been, but health reform is starting to bring them in line.

- **Enrolling in a government-sponsored coverage option:** Starting in 2014, if you earn less than 133 percent of the Federal Poverty Level, you may qualify for Medicaid.

Consider alternatives to staying on a parent's plan. As previously noted, if you're going to school in another state, coverage under a parent's plan may not be a good idea. Many health insurance plans only provide the highest level of coverage when you use their network of preferred doctors and hospitals. Those networks may not extend out of state. Even if you're studying in-state, you should get quotes for individual plans, and compare that to how much it costs to stay on or enroll in your parents' health insurance plan. You may be able to find more affordable coverage with benefits that still meet your needs.

Understand the benefits (and risks) of buying coverage on your own. Check out your individual health insurance options, especially if you're going to school in a different state and your parents' plan won't cover you. Work with a licensed agent like eHealthInsurance.com to compare quotes. As a result of the health reform law, individual plans now provide more robust benefits and access to more preventive care at no out-of-pocket cost. Depending on where you live, your health history, and what kind of coverage you want, you may find some affordable options; Mom and Dad may even help you cover the premiums. But be aware that until 2014 you can still be turned down for individual coverage based on a pre-existing medical condition.

Be sure your health insurance plan covers school sports injuries. NCAA rules often require college athletes to have health insurance, but they don't necessarily require your school to cover you. If you're still insured under your parents' health insurance plan, be aware that some plans may actually exclude coverage for college sports-related injuries. Make sure you understand how your coverage works before you hit the field.

Don't let yourself fall through the cracks as an older student. Undergraduates and graduate students age 26 and older do not qualify to stay on their parents' health insurance plans, even if they are in school on a full-time basis. The health-care reform law limits that option to younger adults. So, if you're age 26 or older—or if you're going to turn 26 in the middle of the academic year—it's a good idea to explore other health insurance alternatives now.

IMPORTANT THINGS TO REMEMBER

- It's becoming increasingly common for employers to require you to submit applications online, so you should have copies of your resume and related materials stored on your computer.

- Your school may have a variety of resources available to help you in your job search, so be sure to ask.

- There is a difference, possibly a big one, between the amount you earn and the amount you will actually receive in your paycheck.

- In addition to salary, there are other things such as health insurance and other benefits you must consider when contemplating a job offer.

Chapter Seven: Budgeting and Saving

One of the most important money-related skills is learning how to spend and save wisely. This is something that doesn't come easily for many people. In fact, many adults who have been working for years and have lots of experience handling money still have trouble spending it in a smart way and being responsible about saving it. Often, a big part of the problem is lack of impulse control. People become accustomed to buying something whenever they get the urge, without taking the time to consider whether they really need the item and, more important, whether they can afford it. This leads to overspending and getting into debt, and it may possibly cause bigger problems if you spend money that you need for important things like rent and other bills.

Envelope System

Years ago when people paid for everything in cash, many used the "envelope system"—where on payday they took their stack of cash and divided it up into a bunch of envelopes, each marked for a specific purpose, such as groceries, rent or mortgage, and utilities. It was a system that kept many folks financially on track and on top of their hard earned dollars, yet most of us today would hardly find this very practical. But no worries! The envelope system has been updated to modern world. There are now numerous online versions that may also include mobile apps for Android and iPhone. You can simply *Google* "Envelope System Online Free," or check out these sites. Note, however, that there may be a monthly fee following a free "trial" period:

- https://www.eebacanhelp.com
- http://www.mvelopes.com/
- https://neobudget.com/
- http://MySpendingPlan.com

CREATING A BUDGET

The best way to handle money wisely is to create a budget, and then stick to it. A budget is a plan for how you will spend your money in the smartest way. In order to create a budget, you must know how much money you have coming in, and then come up with a strategy for where you will spend it.

If you have a job with steady hours and a paycheck that stays roughly the same every payday, then you should have a basic idea of how much money you have coming in every month. It's the other part of the equation—establishing how you will spend the money—that usually is much more difficult.

Actually, creating a budget generally isn't that difficult. It's sticking to a budget that can be tough. It's easy to say that you will use most of your paycheck to pay bills, but then if you take a trip to the mall and see something you really want, you may forget all about those bills you intended to pay.

That's why budgeting requires not only organization and good math skills, but it also requires self-discipline and impulse control.

EXPERT ADVICE

How to Survive on a Budget Through the Year at College:
1. Plan on spending $100 a week on miscellaneous expenses during each semester, and plan on this as part of your summer job college savings goals. To manage your expenses for one year of college, plan on 32 weeks of savings at $100 a week for the year—you will need about $3,200 to safely get you through.
2. Spread purchases throughout the summer before starting school so that you don't need to make one expensive trip to stores such as Target or Wal-Mart. Laundry detergent, toiletries, linens, towels, food, school supplies—all these things add up, and money can be saved by spreading out the purchases and utilizing coupons and other discounts.

From American Consumer Credit Counseling

SETTING UP YOUR BUDGET

There is no one "right" way to set up a budget. There are lots of different systems and techniques for creating one. You could go with the old-fashioned system of using a ledger or accounting book or even just a regular notebook or chart. Or you can go high-tech and use some of the websites or online tools that make it easy for you to create a fancy budget with lots of cool design elements. Or you could do something in between, maybe creating a basic Excel spreadsheet. In the Resources section at the end of this book, we've included a list of websites and other tools that might be helpful to you in creating a budget.

The main thing is that you just create the budget. You can use whatever format you wish. Just pick something that is comfortable for you. If you try to get too fancy or complicated, it may quickly become overwhelming to maintain, and you are more likely to give up. It might be a good idea to start out with something simple just to get comfortable with the basic idea of a budget, and then gradually expand your system as you get used to it.

Next, you'll find a sample budget worksheet from Nelnet, an education planning and financing company, which may work for you.

BUDGET WORKSHEET

It's easy to prepare a budget. Common categories are included in this worksheet, just fill in the amount you typically spend in the budget column. Use the actual column to record spending to see if your budget is on target or needs to be adjusted—check your bill statements and receipts for the most accurate numbers.

Monthly Expenses	Budget	Actual	Monthly Expenses	Budget	Actual
Deductions			**Personal and Health**		
Savings (to be set aside)	$	$	Clothing	$	$
Child Support/Alimony	$	$	Toiletries/Care Products	$	$
Other:	$	$	Haircuts	$	$
Housing			Monthly Dues/Fees	$	$
Rent/Mortgage Payment	$	$	Insurance (Health, Life)	$	$
Utilities (Gas, Water, Electric)	$	$	Doctor/Dentist Visits	$	$
Home Insurance and Taxes	$	$	Prescriptions/OTC Drugs	$	$
HOA Fees	$	$	Laundry/Dry Cleaning	$	$
Other:	$	$	Other:	$	$
Debt Payment			**Education**		
Credit Cards Payments	$	$	Tuition	$	$
Student Loans	$	$	Books/Fees	$	$
Other:	$	$	Supplies	$	$
Food			Other:	$	$
Groceries	$	$	**Entertainment**		
Eating Out/Fast Food	$	$	Concerts/Movies	$	$
Campus Meal Plan	$	$	Sporting Events	$	$
Other:	$	$	Sports/Recreation Equipment	$	$
Transportation			DVDs, CDs, Video Games	$	$
Car Payment	$	$	Other:	$	$
License and Registration	$	$	**Miscellaneous/Unexpected**		
Gas/Oil	$	$	Gifts/Charity	$	$
Normal Car Maintenance	$	$	Pet Supplies/Vet	$	$
Public Transit, Parking, Toll	$	$	Traffic Ticket	$	$
Other:	$	$	Car Repair	$	$
Family			Home Repair/Improvement	$	$
Day Care/Babysitting	$	$	Entertaining Guests	$	$
Activities/Lessons	$	$	Other:	$	$
Pet Sitting	$	$	**Monthly Net Income**	$	$
Other:	$	$	- Total Expenses (from above)	$	$
			= **Monthly Spendable Income**	$	$

EDUCATION LOAN
SERVICING

As a college student, you are probably very comfortable using technology and working with online tools. So you may like using an online system such as Mint.com to create and maintain your budget. An online system can have several advantages. First, it makes it pretty easy to keep things neat and organized. Also, the system usually does the math for you, so you don't need to worry about doing any calculations.

In addition, an online system can provide information and insights. For example, it can show you the percentage of your income that you spend on a particular item or category—clothing, for example. Odds are, you will be surprised at where some of your money goes.

Whatever system you choose, the basic steps are the same. First, you record all of your income: the paycheck from your job, any "side income" you may have (from tutoring, babysitting, or other jobs), and any money you receive from your parents or other sources. If your income fluctuates from month to month, it's best to estimate on the lower end, just to be safe. The total amount you have coming in every month is your income. This is the amount you have available to use for all of your expenses. The second part of the process is to divide up this money and plan where it will go. Obviously, the first priority are rent, utilities, and other fixed expenses—expenses that remain fairly consistent every month, such as your phone bill, along with any school-related bills you may have.

TIP

If you tend to have difficulty being disciplined with your money and have trouble resisting the temptation to spend it on "fun stuff," you should consider setting up automatic bill payments. This is where the amount due on a certain bill is automatically deducted from your bank account. Basically, the money goes out of your available funds before you ever get your hands on it, so you don't have a chance to spend it on anything else.

You want to list your expenses in terms of importance. Obviously, the essential expenses are your top priority and should be at the top of the list. As you go along, you may have to try and make some tough decisions about what should be a priority, especially if you are on a tight budget. For example, cable television is nice to have, but it isn't a necessity.

WHEN YOUR OUTGOING IS GREATER THAN YOUR INCOMING

If you create a budget and find that your expenses are more than your income, you obviously have a problem. That math just won't work. It's impossible to have more going out than you have coming in, and if you find yourself in this situation, you may end up making some unpleasant and probably unwise moves, like using credit cards to pay for groceries and other basic needs, or borrowing from friends or relatives even though you have no way to repay them.

To avoid that, you must evaluate your situation and carefully consider your options. This will take some time and thought. You probably have a few options. The most obvious is to cut some of your expenses. In some cases, there may be some obvious things you can trim from your budget—splurges and nonessentials. Study your expenses closely. There may be relatively painless ways that you can trim things from your budget. Often, just by being a smart consumer you can cut quite a bit from your expenses. For example, you may be able to drop some optional features from your phone plan, or you might be able to negotiate a better rate with your cable company if you've been a long-time customer. We'll give more suggestions on saving money later in this chapter.

Most likely, this will be an extended process. You will probably need to keep returning to your list of expenses and study one item at a time, considering ways you can lower a particular cost. The idea is to keep tweaking those figures until you eventually meet your goal—balancing your budget so that the math works out evenly, allowing your income to cover all of your expenses.

Of course, sometimes no matter how hard you try or how well you cut your expenses, the math just doesn't add up. This is especially likely if you do not make much, and therefore don't have much income with which to work. Even a very smart shopper can only stretch a tiny paycheck so far. In this case, you may have to think about bigger—and perhaps more drastic—solutions. For example, you may need to look for a job that pays better, or add another part-time job, although that might be difficult or impossible, depending on your school schedule and other commitments.

Or you may need to look for a less expensive apartment or reduce your housing costs by getting a roommate. Obviously, this doesn't apply if you already live at home. But if you don't live at home, moving back in with your parents may be something you need to consider if you are struggling to afford your own place.

Andrew Schrage of MoneyCrashers.com says it's essential that college students and 20-somethings get on a budget. He notes, "They're normally out on their own for the first time, and more than likely managing their own finances for the first time. A personal budget is the starting point for financial success, and creating one is simple: write out your income on one side of a page and all monthly expenses on the other. Include amounts for annual expenses if there are any, such as auto insurance premiums. The first goal is to get spending to be less than income. That can be accomplished by reducing monthly services such as Internet, cell phone, and cable TV by either investigating the competition or bundling services. Coupon clipping will save a ton at the grocery store as well."

Schrage adds, "Once that's done, the young adult has three main financial areas they should consider devoting any surplus to: credit card or student loan debt, an emergency fund, or saving for retirement. The debts are the first ones to get out of the way, but not to the exclusion of an emergency fund or retirement savings. If the young adult focuses on saving, they can all be addressed simultaneously, albeit it in a smaller fashion, until all debts are paid off. Then the goal should be nine months' worth of living expenses in an emergency fund and then saving as much as possible for retirement.

Some of the additional mistakes that college students and 20-somethings should steer clear from include making extravagant purchases right out of college. This generally occurs because they're not used to handling a weekly salary, especially if it's rather large. Instead, young adults should choose either a smaller-sized item or an earlier model. If there's a 90-inch flat screen TV available, go with a 50-inch instead. If the iPad 5 just hit the market, choose an iPad 3 or 4."

For more information, check out these sites:

http://www.moneycrashers.com/how-to-make-a-budget/

http://www.moneycrashers.com/reduce-avoid-student-loan-debt/

http://www.moneycrashers.com/start-build-emergency-fund-savings/

SHORT-TERM SOLUTIONS FOR CASH SHORTAGES

No matter how well we budget, there are times when things don't go according to plan. Sometimes you may find yourself experiencing an unexpected money crisis due to an emergency or unplanned bill—say, if your car breaks down or you have a medical emergency that requires an ER visit.

Ideally, you will have some savings or an emergency fund that you can use to get through this money crunch. But for most college students, accumulating a "rainy day fund" can be tough. If you don't have any available savings, then you need to figure out another way to come up with some quick cash.

The good news is, if you think about it hard enough, you can probably come up with a few ideas, especially if you think creatively. If you have any particular skills or talents, you may be able to use them to generate some income. For example, you could give music lessons, design web pages, or set up a wireless network for someone. To find people who need help with these kinds of things, you can post notices on local bulletin boards or just spread the word via your social networks.

Another option is to think about things you can sell. Chances are, you have some stuff you no longer use or don't want, especially if you look at the stuff in your attic or the back of your closet. You might be surprised at how much you can get for these things, especially if the items are in good shape or are possibly collectibles. Things like baseball cards, old toys, and anything that's rare or hard to find may be worth more than you think. You can take them to a sports shop, antique store, or a business that buys collectibles and see what they offer you. Or you can sell them online on Ebay or a similar site.

Websites such as CraigsList that let you post "for sale" ads at no cost may give you the opportunity to sell the items more quickly because you can find a local buyer. However, these sites tend to attract a large number of scam artists and people who may try to take advantage of you, so you need to use caution and always meet a potential buyer in a public place. Also, it's best to require payment in cash. A common scam involves the buyer sending you a money order that turns out to be fake, which you don't discover until you've already given them the item.

If you have electronics you don't want, there are a few ways you can get money for them. With video games, gaming systems, or accessories, you may be able to sell them at a local video game store. You can sell other "gadgets" such as iPods at sites like NextWorth or Gazelle.

Amazon.com also has programs where you can sell electronics, DVDs, games, books, and other items easily through their website.

TIP

Don't forget about your change! If you have a stash of coins somewhere, you can "cash them in" for dollar bills (or gift cards, in some cases) at a machine like Coinstar. And be sure to check your coat pockets, purses—and yes, under the couch cushions. Most likely you can find quite a bit of change all over your apartment. And you might be surprised at how quickly that change can add up! Some coin-counting machines will charge a fee, which is usually a certain percentage of the total value of your coins. However, some banks also have coin-counting machines that you can use for free if you deposit that money into your account.

TIPS FOR STICKING TO YOUR BUDGET

As we've already said, creating a budget is the easy part. Sticking to your budget, on the other hand, isn't always so easy. You may have good intentions at the beginning of the month, but a few weeks later, you may wonder why you're already broke even though you haven't paid all of your bills yet.

TRACK YOUR SPENDING

One of the biggest problems with spending your money wisely is that often you don't know exactly where your money goes. If you've ever found yourself out of money even though it doesn't feel like you have anything to show for it, you need to figure out exactly how you are spending your money.

A good way to do this is to keep a spending journal. For a week (or, better yet, a month), write down every single thing you buy. This includes small or minor purchases, like a cup of coffee or a magazine. Then study the total amount you have spent on each item. Most likely, this will be an eye-opening experience. Many of us don't realize how much we spend on little things. Common areas where we kill our budget include quick purchases on the way to or from work or school (coffee, snacks, etc.) and entertainment or social activities. If you meet up with friends at night for something to eat or to see a movie—that can cost more than you might think.

When you look at your total purchases for the week or month, you will likely see a few places where you are spending way more than you planned. Of course, the next question is, now that you have that information, what do you do about it? Well, the obvious answer is that you need to somehow reduce or eliminate this spending. But that may be easier said than done.

AUTOMATE YOUR PAYMENTS

By setting up an automatic payment arrangement, you can make sure those bills get paid before you have a chance to spend that money on something else. This also helps you avoid any late fees or other problems if you forget to pay the bill on time.

FACTOR IN SOME FUN MONEY

If at all possible, include at least a small amount that is designated as "fun money" that you can use for whatever you want. Even if this isn't much, it will give you something to spend in a way you enjoy. This will help you feel a bit less deprived, which may help you resist the urge to splurge.

EXPERT ADVICE

Certified Financial Planner Leah Manderson says learning how to be responsible with money isn't just about dollars and cents, and it takes more than a knack for finding bargains. She notes, "While taking these actions will get you to your goal, the real test is psychological. To manage your money psychologically, start to identify yourself as the type of person who is financially responsible, enjoys simplicity, values experiences over things, practices gratitude, and who buys based on value (over price, status, etc.)."

Visit www.leahmanderson.com/ for more information.

STRATEGIES FOR SAVING MONEY

One of the best ways to help your budget is to figure out ways that you can save money on some of your major types of expenses. Here are some quick tips for cutting costs:

TRANSPORTATION

- See if you can stay on your parents' car insurance. It will probably be cheaper than getting your own policy.

- Better yet, consider whether you need a car at all—at least, whether you need one with you all the time. If you live on or near campus, it may be cheaper, not to mention more convenient, to leave your car at your parents' house. Most large campuses and major cities have lots of public transportation options. This way, you save the cost of parking and the hassle of trying to find parking spaces. And for times when you do need a car, you may be able to use Zipcar or a similar service. These car-renting services are targeting college students and therefore opening many new locations near large campuses.

- Use an app like GasBuddy to find the cheapest gas prices in your area.

123

TECHNOLOGY

- Apple, Adobe, and other major tech companies offer special educational pricing or student discounts on certain products.

- Buy used and refurbished items on eBay or Amazon.

- Sell your unwanted gadgets on sites like NextWorth or Gazelle, where you can earn credit toward a newer model.

- Get a computer lock so you can fasten your laptop to your desk or other location, making it less likely to be stolen.

MUSIC AND MOVIES

- Watch television shows or movies online at Crackle, Hulu, or Netflix.

- Listen to music free through streaming radio or online music sites like Pandora.

- If your parents have DIRECTV or HBO at home, they also get free access to this programming online, which they will probably let you use while you're at school.

- With an Amazon Prime account, you get free two-day shipping on most items, including DVDs. You can also get unlimited instant video streaming. Best of all, students get a free six-month membership!

TIP

There's no need to drive all over town to get the best bargains. Most major stores will "price match." This means that if you bring in an ad from a competing store showing an item at a less expensive price, that store will sell you the item for that same price.

FOOD AND DRINKS

- Instead of buying bottled water, invest in a filter and drink tap water.

- Use coupons. Yes, we know it seems old-fashioned, but coupons can really save you a lot of money. And you don't necessarily have to buy the Sunday newspaper to get the coupons. There are plenty of online coupon sites like Coupons.com or CouponCabin.com where you can print coupons.

- Be careful when you go out to eat with a large group. Some restaurants automatically add a specific gratuity charge to large parties. Also, if everyone decides to "split the check," you can come out on the bad end of the deal if you carefully choose an affordable option, but everyone else buys expensive food and drinks.

In 2012, re:fuel, a leading marketing firm, released its *College Explorer* study, the largest study of its kind to take a comprehensive look at many aspects of campus life—from spending habits to tech usage. Here are some interesting stats from that study:

Students in 2012 spent more than $44 billion on total food expenses, including $20.7 billion in grocery stores, $9.6 billion on food at convenience stores, and $13.7 billion dining out. Of the students surveyed about their spending habits in a typical month, 92 percent said they visit off-campus grocery stores, 88 percent visit quick-service restaurants, and 83 percent visit sit-down restaurants.

STUDENT ADVICE

Pack a lunch to bring to school, since cafeteria food is outrageous. Also, if bus transportation is available, take the bus instead of putting gas into your vehicle. Walk from building to building on campus instead of driving to different buildings for class.

~Brittany Y., Pennsylvania

125

ENLIST THE HELP OF THE ONLINE COMMUNITY

You use online communities and social networks for pretty much everything else, so why not use them to help you save money? There are lots of forums and communities for bargain hunters and smart shoppers. On these forums, people share lots of great resources, such as coupon codes, online deals, tips on finding bargains, and lots of other helpful information.

Here are a few bargain-hunting sites to check out:

www.FatWallet.com

www.SlickDeals.net

www.BigBigForums.com

TIP

Before buying anything online, do a web search for the item name or brand and the word "coupon" or "coupon code." There's a good chance you'll be able to find a coupon code that will let you get a discount on an item that you are looking to purchase.

Financial attorney and debt specialist Leslie Tayne, Esq., (http://www.attorney-newyork.com/) shares some of the biggest budget mistakes young people make:

- **Not knowing how much you actually make:** If you don't know how much you earn, you have no way of knowing what your spending limit should be. This can result in overspending and can trigger a dangerous habit that not only can be hard to break but may also lead you toward a dangerous path of endless debt.

- **Not understanding that you need to have enough generated each month to cover your expenses:** If you do not know how much you have to pay on a monthly basis, you will not know your spending limit, which could result in overspending and a larger debt-to-income ratio.

- **Moving out of your house too soon:** Don't jump the gun in fleeing the nest before you are financially ready. Make sure a move fits into your budget and that you account for not only rent but also any maintenance and utilities.

- **Having no savings or back up for emergencies:** In a case of an emergency, you may find yourself resorting to the use of a credit card if you don't have any fall-back savings set aside for emergency situations, which could leave you inheriting high-interest debt that you will have to pay back.

Ilene Davis, CFP®, M.B.A., offers two simple steps for getting started on your budget skills:

1. For three months, do not spend on anything that is not a necessary bill or necessary for BASIC survival.

2. Carry a small notebook for three months, and write down EVERYTHING spent.

Davis recommends that you do these two things to become truly familiar with what money you spend and to help you curb impulse spending. Then she suggests that you read *The Richest Man in Babylon*, by George S. Clason, and follow at least his first three rules: pay yourself first, control your expenses, and put your money to work.

She adds, "Anyone who wants to be financially independent can find a way to save at least $5 a day. It's not enough for full retirement, but it's a good place to start. I have clients get an empty 2-liter soda bottle and put in at least $1 a day, preferably $5, and watch their money grow. After two months, they should have enough to start a systematic investment plan with $100/month."

Elle Kaplan, CEO & Founding Partner of Lexion Capital Management, says you may need to work at getting yourself in the habit of sticking to a budget. "If necessary, a 'cash-only diet' can be very helpful in establishing healthy money management habits. Unlike with plastic, you can't easily overspend—you withdraw the amount you have in your budget for that week, and when it's gone it's gone. Don't fall into the easily-avoidable trap of credit card debt. I see a lot of grads with a "pay for it later" mindset, and that needs to be adjusted. If you can't afford buy it outright, don't charge it. It's not about depriving yourself of everything fun. It's about taking control of your financial life—and that's something to feel great about."

THE 50/20/30 RULE

According to Kimberly Foss, CFP, personal finance expert and President of Empyrion Wealth Management, "the big items like rent and utilities or core expenses should be allocated in physical envelopes (or as my 21-year-old daughter does, in mason jars decorated with names on the lids— rent, transportation, food, etc.). Once you have the physical container, you add the actual green dollars for the month to each jar, and only use those physical dollars for that expense."

After that, Foss suggests you try the **50/20/30 Rule**, which involves efficiently breaking down everyday costs by their spending order and importance. Here are the three categories:

- **Essential Expenses—50 percent** of your take-home pay should go toward the necessities (housing, utilities, and food).

- **Financial priorities—20 percent** (at least) should be allocated for essential financial needs, such as savings accounts or paying off debt.

- **Lifestyle choices—30 percent** of your take-home pay should be spent on personal lifestyle choices (entertainment, shopping, dining out, and so on). This is the last priority when budgeting.

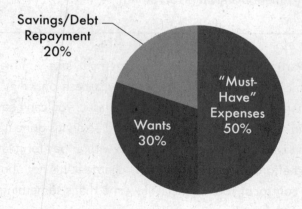

Your Monthly Income

FIVE TIPS FOR SMARTER SPENDING

1. **Resist impulse buying (or at least reduce your ability to do it).** If you know you have little willpower when it comes to shopping, avoid the mall or other places where you are likely to splurge. Or try to find enough room in your budget for a small amount that can be designated as your fun spending fund, and limit yourself to impulse buys that are within that amount.

2. **Shop around.** Before making a purchase—especially if it's for something large or expensive—be sure to comparison shop to make sure you're getting the best deal. This is very easy to do online, as there are many price comparison websites that will show you the best prices.

3. **Keep a money journal.** Carefully record every single penny you spend for an entire week or month. Chances are you will be surprised at where your money goes. This can help you spot places where you can cut back or change your spending habits.

4. **Being a bargain-hunter can be cool.** There's nothing wrong with being a savvy shopper. And don't be embarrassed to use coupons or wait for sales. Just think about all the great stuff you can buy with the money you will save!

5. **Use cash whenever possible.** It's easy to lose track of exactly how much you are spending when you use plastic. By handing over your hard-earned dollars for every purchase, you will better realize just where your money is going.

IMPORTANT THINGS TO REMEMBER

- Living on a budget may not always be fun, but it will pay off in the long run by helping you enjoy a financially stable future.

- With a little effort and research, you can usually find ways to cut down on many of your major expenses.

- Coupons, online deal sites, and bargain-hunting forums can all be valuable resources in helping you save money.

Chapter Eight: Identity Theft, Fraud, and Other Scams

Learning how to earn, spend, and save money wisely is an important part of financial know-how. Once you have money, you need to keep it safe. The same goes for your good credit, which is a valuable asset. This is why you need to educate yourself about identity theft and other types of scams and fraud.

Understanding Identity Theft

As you can probably guess from the name, identity theft is basically when someone steals your identity or your personal information. They then use it to steal your money or establish credit in your name.

Types of Identity Theft

Identity theft can take many forms. The thief may literally impersonate you—say, by going to a car dealership and obtaining a loan by pretending to be you. But it's far more common for someone just to use your name, account numbers, or other personal information.

A common scenario is that the thief will open an account using your name but will have the credit card or purchased items sent to their address; often, this will be a post office box or a shipping store where he/she can rent a mailbox.

Or the scammer may get a hold of your credit card, or just the numbers from your credit card or bank account, and use it to make purchases, get cash advances, or withdraw money from your bank account.

Criminals come up with many creative ways to commit identity theft. They may even use your name to get a job or to obtain medical treatment.

This is why it is so important for you to be diligent about monitoring the activity on your bank or credit accounts. It's a good idea to just do a quick check online on a daily basis. Be sure to notify your bank or credit card company immediately if you see any transactions you don't recognize or if you spot any other signs of suspicious activity.

TIP

Don't ignore a mysterious charge or transaction just because it is for a tiny amount. This is a common tactic used by crooks. They will do a "test run," charging a small amount at first just to see if the account is active—and also to see if anyone is paying attention. Once they get away with this initial attempt, they will soon follow it up with a much larger transaction.

PROTECTING YOURSELF FROM IDENTITY THEFT

These days, with so much of our information easily available online and via other sources, it can be tough to protect yourself completely against identity theft. But there are some steps you can take to reduce your odds of becoming a target.

- **Use strong passwords.** Avoid using very obvious things, like your pet's name. Ideally, you should use a combination of letters and numbers, symbols, or other characters.

- **Guard your cards and information.** This probably seems obvious, but it's important to be very careful about where and how you use your credit cards and personal information. Be cautious about sharing your Social Security number or other personal/financial details. Be especially leery of sharing your information online—unless it is a secure (https) website.

- **Don't share too much.** Think twice about revealing personal details in your social media profiles. Things like your birthdate, city where you were born, mother's maiden name—these are all details that can help a crook steal your identity or guess the answers to your security questions.

- **Invest in a shredder.** You can get a basic inexpensive model at an office supply store. Use it to shred any credit card offers, bank statements, or other mail and documents that contain your personal information.

- **Use one-time-only credit card numbers.** Many banks and credit card companies now offer a way for you to get a special credit card number that is only valid for one use, or for a certain amount of time. This is especially helpful if you want to purchase something online, particularly if it's from a website you haven't used before. By making your purchase using a one-time card number, you prevent scammers from accessing your main account.

- **Put a fraud alert on your credit files.** This requires that a bank, credit card company, or other financial entity take extra steps for verification whenever anyone other than you tries to open an account or obtain credit in your name. The downside is that it will be a little more of a hassle for you whenever you want to open accounts because, of course, you will have to prove that you are, in fact, actually you, but it's worth the minor inconvenience to keep your identity and credit safe.

- **Check your credit reports often.** Look for inaccuracies as well as accounts or credit information you don't recognize. As we mentioned earlier in this book, you are entitled to a free copy of your credit report from each of the three major credit bureaus once per year.

- **Consider a credit monitoring service.** These services—available through places like Credit Karma and LifeLock—send you an alert whenever new credit accounts are opened in your name or when there is some change to your credit history/profile.

SCAMMING TRICKS

BEWARE OF NAME-DROPPING

Scammers will often use clever tricks to get you to let your guard down and trust them. One such tactic is claiming they know someone close to you. For example, they may send you an e-mail that opens with, "I can only offer this secret deal to a select group of people, but since John Smith is a friend of mine, he asked me to include you."

The problem is—and this may be an eye-opening and somewhat disturbing fact—it's very easy for a complete stranger to find out who your friends and relatives are, simply by browsing through your "friends" or contacts list on social media sites.

PHISHING

Phishing is becoming very common, and it is one of the top ways that scammers get their hands on your accounts and personal information. Phishing is a term that basically means using some kind of online scam, like a phony e-mail or a bogus website, to trick you into revealing your information. Rather than going through a lot of effort to steal your information, the crooks just fool you into handing it over.

Phishing, like many other common scams today, involves some sort of **social engineering**—the process of manipulating or tricking you into doing a certain action or revealing information. Usually this involves some sort of interaction that plays upon common human nature—such as the desire to want to help someone who seems to be in distress or the urge to give in to the temptation to get free money or merchandise.

HOW IT WORKS

Generally, in a phishing scam, you will receive some sort of e-mail or text that looks and sounds very official and urgent. It will usually appear to be sent by a bank, a credit card company, or even a government agency like the IRS.

The Federal Trade Commission offers these examples:

- "We suspect an unauthorized transaction on your account. To ensure that your account is not compromised, please click the link below and confirm your identity."
- "During our regular verification of accounts, we couldn't verify your information. Please click here to update and verify your information."
- "Our records indicate that your account was overcharged. You must call us within seven days to receive your refund."

Usually, the message will contain a link or URL that you are instructed to use in order to check on your account or verify your information.

If you click the link, you will see a website that looks official. That's because the scammer has copied it from the real bank page or other official source. However, what you don't realize is that you aren't actually on an official bank or business website. Instead, you are actually on a phony website the scammer has created. Once you enter your account information, the scammer will then quickly use that to access your account, where they will immediately change the password and contact information, thus locking you out of your own account while they clear out your funds, charge items to your account, or do their other dirty work.

Sometimes these e-mails will also include a phone number for you to call. This is just another part of the scam—the phone number is often a foreign number, which will end up costing you huge phone charges.

SAMPLE SCAMS

While there are countless different types of scams out there (crooks can be very creative!), there are some common ploys that scammers use frequently.

THE NIGERIAN SCAM

This type of scam got its name because initially many of the scam e-mails of this type originated from Nigeria, but today they've spread all over the globe. The basic scenario goes like this: A wealthy foreigner is fleeing persecution or belongs to a ruling family whose regime is being overthrown. He's stashed a fortune somewhere, and he needs your help moving it to America or elsewhere. He promises you a hefty sum for your assistance. Of course, he will need your bank account information in order to transfer this money to you. Once you hand that over, he will disappear, along with as much of your money as he can get.

THE LONG-LOST RELATIVE SCAM

In this scenario, you are contacted by someone claiming to be an attorney, financial manager, or other representative handling the estate of a wealthy person who recently passed away. It's your lucky day, because apparently you have turned out to be the long-lost heir of this person you honestly don't know and have never heard of before!

135

THE "FRIEND OR RELATIVE IN TROUBLE" SCAM

With this scam, you receive an urgent text or e-mail that appears to be coming from a friend or relative. He or she is experiencing some sort of emergency—often it involves having their wallet stolen while far away from home—and needs your help to pay the hotel bill or to get back home. You're asked to send some money via Western Union or a similar method. Of course, this "friend or relative" promises to repay you immediately as soon as he or she gets home and can straighten things out. The problem is that this message isn't coming from your friend or family member; it's coming from a scammer who has managed to make it look like the message is coming from a certain phone number or e-mail address.

HOW TO PROTECT YOURSELF FROM COMPUTER-BASED SCAMS

• Use strong passwords, and change them often.

• Never click on links contained in e-mails claiming to be from your bank, credit card company, or other organization. Instead, to check any alerts or updates about your account, go to the company's website by typing in the URL yourself, not by clicking on an e-mail link.

• Don't send personal information such as your Social Security number or bank/credit account numbers via e-mail.

• The IRS and other government or law enforcement agencies will <u>never</u> contact you about an investigation or request personal information via e-mail. These agencies would get in touch with you by phone, snail mail, or in person.

• Be very cautious about opening any attachments or downloading information you receive via e-mail.

• Make sure you have a good antivirus program installed on your computer, and update it regularly.

Another tip: Take advantage of "double verification" safeguards. In an attempt to make it tougher for scammers to hijack someone's account or steal their information, many websites and social media services have started enacting two-step verification processes. This means, for example, that in order to change or recover your password, you will need to enter a code that will be sent to your phone number. The specific steps involved can vary. This is extra security to prevent someone from easily taking control of your account. In some cases, this is an optional feature—you have a choice of whether to use it. You should always take advantage of this, if it is offered. It's a very small inconvenience that can have great benefits.

SMISHING

Smishing is similar to phishing, only the scammers contact you via text messages to your phone. You will receive a text message that appears to be from a person or company you know, and it asks you to provide personal information by calling a phone number or clicking on a link, where you will be taken to a fake website that—just as with phishing—may look like the real website of a legitimate company.

As with phishing, the best way to protect yourself is by not clicking or responding to any messages that request your personal information. If you want to find out if that a bank or business is really trying to reach you, contact them directly by looking up their number yourself —don't call the number in the e-mail.

SPYWARE AND OTHER NASTY COMPUTER THREATS

Sometimes, scammers will send you an e-mail, but they don't care if you actually click on any links on it. That's because the e-mail itself is the dangerous part of this scam. The e-mail will likely contain an attachment that is loaded with spyware, a virus, or other bad stuff that will track your computer activities, including any passwords or other information you type, or it will just cause you a lot of computer problems.

VIDEO GAME AND SOCIAL MEDIA SCAMS

An area of fraud/scamming that's exploding involves using video games or social media to lure in victims or gain access to their information. While the particular tactics can vary, here's one common scenario:

You're in the middle of playing an online game—this could be through a console system like Xbox Live or an online-based game—and suddenly someone (either another player or someone posing as a moderator or other "official" game representative) will offer you a way to earn a lot of extra points, rewards, or special bonuses. This individual may tell you this is because you've reached a certain elite level, or it's simply because you were lucky enough to be chosen at random.

Just as with phishing, you are directed to click on something in order to claim your bonus. As soon as you do that, the scammer immediately hijacks your account. From there, he/she can do all sorts of things ranging from something annoying, like playing games while posing as you, to something more serious, such as charging purchases to the credit card you have on file or creating offensive posts while using your online identity.

Again, the best way to avoid becoming a victim is by not clicking on links. Yes, it can be tough to resist the urge to claim some cool bonus items, but remember the old saying—if it seems too good to be true it probably is.

Also, be suspicious of any links you may get in direct messages on Twitter, Facebook, or similar social media sites.

5 TIPS FOR PROTECTING YOUR INFORMATION ON SOCIAL MEDIA

By Mark Seguin, Founder and CEO of TBG Solutions—training and resources to help protect against identity theft

1. **Remove your birthday and hometown from Facebook.** A study out of Carnegie Mellon University discovered that with just your birthday and hometown, there is a formula that can predict the first five digits of your Social Security number. It's accurate almost 50 percent of the time! And what do you give everyone else over the phone for a security code? Answer: the last four digits of your Social Security number.

2. **Limit the amount of personal information that you put on your profile.** This includes the following: address, family members, and pets' names. We often use this information as our security words, passwords, or for personal identification questions. Don't put it out there for the world to see!

3. **Never post photos or status updates that give away your current location.** If you are posting about your trip to Disney World, then where are you NOT currently? Home! This is an opportune time for thieves to break in and steal from your house.

4. **Be wary of online surveys.** They could be legitimate websites trying to gather marketing data about you, or they could be identity thieves posing as legitimate businesses.

5. **Don't be an easy target.** Use the tightest possible privacy settings on each social network. Make sure that only your friends are seeing your posts—not the public. However, remember that any site can be hacked and broken through, so don't be careless with what you post even if your privacy is locked down tightly.

OTHER TYPES OF SCAMS

CALLER ID SPOOFING

While the Internet is a popular method for many scams today, some crooks still rely on the phone to try to rip you off. One effective tactic is Caller ID spoofing. This is when the crook manipulates the information that shows up on caller ID, making it seem like they are calling from anywhere they choose. So, for example, the phone rings and the caller ID says Publishers Clearing House or the Internal Revenue Service. In reality, it's just someone trying to trick you into revealing personal or financial information.

FAKE MONEY ORDERS

Not long ago, money orders were a popular choice when you wanted to send payment for something via snail mail. Money orders were considered secure and, unlike a personal check, you didn't have to worry about waiting for it to clear or wondering if it would bounce. Recently, though, crooks have taken advantage of the fact that most people trust money orders. Fake money orders are becoming increasingly common. Often, scammers will send you a money order as payment for something you are selling. Once you send them the item, you try to cash or deposit the money order—only to discover that it's phony.

MYSTERY SHOPPING SCAMS

Here's how this scam works: you receive a letter with a nice big check enclosed. The letter appears to be from a mystery shopping company. You're informed that you've been selected to do a mystery shopping job at a store or other business that handles Western Union transactions. You're instructed to cash the check and then use part of the money to send a Western Union transaction—supposedly to test out how the transaction works. Of course, once you've sent out this money, you will later get an urgent call from your bank informing you that the check you deposited was fraudulent, and now you're on the hook for that money.

LOTTERY OR SWEEPSTAKES WINNER SCAM

Winning a contest is exciting, especially if your prize is a large sum of money. So of course you'd be thrilled to get a winning notification in the mail in a fancy envelope from what looks like a legitimate contest agency or lottery organization. You'll rush to do whatever you need to in order to claim your prize. Or at least, that's what the scammer is counting on.

You will be told that you need to send a processing fee or send money toward the taxes due in order to receive your prize.

Here are a few red flags that will help you spot this type of scam:

- Real notifications for large prizes usually come via certified mail, Federal Express, or a similar service.
- You never have to send a payment in order to claim a legitimate prize.
- If you win a large cash prize, your taxes are either deducted from the check or paid with your other tax payments when you file your tax return at the end of the year. You don't need to send a check in advance before receiving your prize.

E-MAILS FROM THE IRS, FBI, AND OTHER SCARY-SOUNDING AGENCIES

Naturally, you would be nervous upon receiving an e-mail from the IRS or a law enforcement agency, especially if it says you are in trouble or are the subject of an urgent investigation. Well, you can breathe a sigh of relief. You can rest assured that if one of these agencies really did want to reach you for an important matter, especially if you were in trouble, the agency wouldn't rely on e-mail to contact you.

HOW FRAUD AND IDENTITY THEFT HAPPEN

As you've learned so far, fraud and identity theft can happen in a variety of ways. Generally, the crook will either steal your information or will somehow trick you into revealing it. He or she may go old-school and use a very simple method like going through your trash—looking for bank statements, credit card offers, or other goldmines of sensitive information. Or, as previously mentioned, thieves can use high-tech methods like phishing or e-mail scams.

The common theme, though, is that they prey on your trusting and open nature, or the fact that you fail to make the effort to guard your private information.

WHY COLLEGE STUDENTS ARE COMMON TARGETS

In some ways, college students, and young people in general, make great targets for scammers and identity thieves. This is due to a few factors common among people of this age group:

- **Inexperience:** Because young people just don't have a lot of experience dealing with financial issues, they may not know what to look for and may overlook some possible red flags.

- **Online sharing:** Young people today share a lot of information online through social networks and other online sources. By paying attention to your posts, updates, and profile information, a smart scammer can get a lot of information that can enable him or her to access your personal information or assume your identity. For example, he or she can determine your location, employer, birthdate, and more. This is another reason why it is so important to put strict privacy controls on your social media accounts and to limit who can see your information.

- **Frequent use of online accounts and plastic:** The more frequently you enter your personal information online, the greater the odds that someone will get his or her hands on it. This is especially true if you do a lot of online shopping at new/unknown websites or those that don't have good security measures in place. Likewise, if you tend to use your credit/debit card a lot at bars, clubs, local stores, restaurants, and other places where your information may be accessed by a lot of people, you are more at risk.

- **Offline theft:** Criminals can also access your information the old-fashioned way: by stealing your wallet, purse, or backpack. Students often leave these things on a desk or the floor in crowded areas, or perhaps unattended in a dorm, where they can be stolen easily. And, of course, an unattended laptop can be a treasure trove of personal information and documents.

IDENTITY PROTECTION TIPS FOR COLLEGE GRADS FROM LIFELOCK

- **Your resume is business, not personal:** Your Social Security number (SSN), date of birth, driver's license number, marital status, full address, professional license number, gender, and age should not be included in your resume. Information such as this can be provided upon request from an employer.

- **Use a unique password for each job search website:** Most job search sites also have privacy settings. Also, make sure you are not sharing too much personal information with employers. It's best to be proactive and look for openings, only sharing personal information when you decide to apply for a job. Research companies on the Internet, and make sure everything corresponds with the information in the ad before responding.

- **Be vigilant**: Look for e-mail addresses that do not contain the domain name of the company. Make sure you research a "want ad" thoroughly before responding. Don't divulge your SSN in your resume or if they call you for a phone interview. Politely ask the interviewer why he or she needs it. Before sending, call the company and make sure the interviewer works there. In most cases, personal information is not relevant until you get to the in-person stage of the interview process.

- **Be proactive with any problematic background checks:** While it occurs later in the interview process, a negative background check can mean an abrupt end of the line. If there are any issues, ask if it's possible to see the results of the background check and look for inaccuracies. You may want to do your own check proactively. If you find any inaccuracies, notify the HR department, and ask for a few days to look into the problem.

- **Keep an eye on your accounts:** It may not be the most uplifting practice to check your bank and credit card accounts regularly. However, the faster you spot wrongful transactions, the less likely you are to be held liable for them.

- **Watch your credit score:** Most recent graduates are just beginning to build credit and aren't concerned with their credit score. But thieves can open credit in your name, which could have disastrous effects down the road. It's important to keep an eye on your credit report, and watch for changes in your score.

- **Ask for this unusual graduation gift:** For peace of mind, consider asking for an identity theft protection service as a graduation gift.

- **Be careful about information you share while networking:** Grads also find themselves spending many evenings at networking events. The same rules apply here, as well, about sharing information to register for and follow up on potential "hot" job opportunities.

P2P FILE SHARING AND SECURITY RISKS

Robert Siciliano, security analyst and identify theft expert, says P2P file sharing poses a particular security risk for young people. He shares the following information:

"Peer-to-peer file sharing, or P2P, has become enormously popular on college campuses across the country because it allows students to easily exchange music and video files over the Internet. Tens of millions of people use P2P applications such as Limewire, eDonkey, and BearShare to fill their MP3 players and hard drives with all the music and movies they want, all for free. But even 'free' has a cost.

In addition to violating copyright laws, there are other potential dangers when downloading files via P2P. For instance, hackers know that source files on P2P networks are not being validated, so it's easy to trick you into downloading a virus or spyware instead of the popular video you thought you were getting.

The other major issue is the simple fact that P2P programs share your data with all of the other P2P users in cyberspace. Because of this, there is a good chance you might unknowingly share your most precious and private data with the rest of the world.

During installation, P2P programs scan your hard drive, looking for files to share. If you do not exercise caution, your entire hard drive, including any confidential documents it may contain, could be left wide open for anyone to access. Think about the files you have on your computer right now. Are you storing documents that have your passwords, Social Security number, or bank account information? If you have P2P software on your PC, you could be targeted for identity theft."

Siciliano notes that while conducting his research on P2P networks, he uncovered tax returns, student loan applications, credit reports, and Social Security numbers. He even found private photos, videos, love letters, and just about anything else that can be saved as a digital file.

He offers the following tips to protect you from accidentally sharing data on a P2P network:

• The smartest way to stay safe is not to install P2P software on your computer in the first place.

• If you think a family member may have installed P2P software on his or her computer, check for any new or unfamiliar applications. A look at your "All Programs Menu" will show nearly every program on your computer. If you see one you don't recognize, do an online search to see if it is a P2P application.

• Set administrative privileges on your computer to prevent the installation of new software without your knowledge.

• Use comprehensive security software such as McAfee® Total Protection, and keep it up to date.

• Make sure your firewall is enabled, and if an application asks you to change your settings to enable access to the Internet, don't allow it.

P2P file sharing can be tempting, but in most cases, the costly dangers just aren't worth it.

IMPORTANT THINGS TO REMEMBER

- Identity theft can happen in a variety of ways, so you need to be always on the lookout for potential scams.

- It's important to protect your personal information and account numbers, because these can be used to steal your identity.

- Think twice about the information you share online or list in your social media profiles.

- Never click on links in e-mails that appear to be from a bank or law enforcement agency.

- Remember the old saying: if it sounds too good to be true, it probably is.

Chapter Nine: Common Mistakes and How to Recover

No matter how careful you are or how much you know about the best ways to handle money responsibly, eventually you will probably make some kind of big financial mistake. Almost all of us have done so at one point or another.

Sometimes it isn't entirely your fault. You may have taken out a loan that you thought you would have no problem paying back—until you lost your job unexpectedly. Or perhaps you suffered an accident or injury that forced you to spend a lot of money on medications and/or doctor bills.

On the other hand, it's possible that you got yourself in a financial mess due entirely to your own actions or careless decisions. If so, don't beat yourself up about it; many people have found themselves in a financial crisis due to impulse buys, poor money management, or other mistakes.

There are some common money mistakes that many people make, so let's review a few of them.

Overspending

One of the most obvious and most common money mistakes is spending too much—more specifically, spending more than you have or more than you can afford.

Overspending usually is related to splurging on clothes, entertainment, travel, or other fun items and experiences. If you see something you want, you may have trouble resisting the urge to buy it. In that moment, you may not take the time to think about how this purchase may affect your financial situation or whether it is in line with your budget.

If you frequently use credit cards to finance your splurges, you may quickly find yourself in hot water. Long after the thrill of that impulse purchase or fun night out has gone, you will be facing credit card bills that you are unable to pay.

If you stick to a cash-only approach, you won't be able to go into a lot of debt through your overspending. But you can still get yourself into a lot of trouble financially, because you may end up spending money that you might need for necessities like rent, food, and school bills.

Of course, the only true solution for overspending is to get control over your spending and stay within your budget limits. But this takes discipline and self-control, and it doesn't always come easy for many people. In fact, people often learn this lesson the hard way—after they've gone through some tough times due to spending their money carelessly.

You can save yourself a lot of stress and headaches by practicing self-control and keeping your spending in check. Yes, this will require you to resist the urge to buy things you want. Self-control isn't always fun, when compared to going on a shopping spree. But the temporary thrill you get from buying that cool gadget or new outfit is short-lived; then you will have to deal with the ramifications of not having the money you need to pay your bills.

There are a few ways to avoid the temptation to overspend:

- **Pay your bills immediately after getting your paycheck.** This will ensure they are taken care of, and it will eliminate your ability to overspend because you won't have that money available.

- **Keep your credit cards out of reach.** If you're on a tight budget, you may have a tendency to view credit as extra spending funds or a way to buy beyond your budget. In reality, relying on credit cards to satisfy your urge to spend is a recipe for disaster. A credit card can be a lifesaver in case of emergency, but it shouldn't be viewed as a magic wand that you can wave whenever you want to go shopping. Keep your credit card in a safe place, but one that isn't too easy for you to access.

- **Designate some fun money in your budget.** Obviously, this might be tough to manage if you have a very tight budget. But giving yourself even just a small amount of "fun money" can keep you from feeling deprived and let you enjoy the feeling of spending a little bit of your money on something you enjoy.

- **Keep your eyes on the goal.** Remind yourself of your priorities and the things you will accomplish by sticking to your budget. This could be the ability to live in your own place or the accomplishment of completing your college degree. By focusing on the "big prize," you will be less likely to be distracted by smaller splurges.

GETTING INTO (TOO MUCH) DEBT

Incurring too much debt is often a result of overspending, but it can also be caused by a variety of other factors. Here are a few examples:

- Borrowing money for school, cars, personal expenses, or other things in an amount that you can't reasonably be sure you will be able to repay
- Engaging in financially risky behavior, such as gambling, where the odds are stacked against you
- Overextending yourself by taking on more expenses than your income will cover
- Failing to plan or prepare for emergencies—say, by failing to obtain insurance or not saving for car repairs

Keep in mind, debt refers to any money you owe to anyone. While this usually refers to credit card companies, banks, and other businesses, it can also mean money you owe to parents, relatives, or friends. Borrowing an excessive amount from loved ones can be just as big a problem as owing that money to a credit card company. In some ways, it's even worse. After all, you don't have to ensure an awkward and uncomfortable family dinner with your credit card company if you've fallen behind on repaying the money you owe.

The basic solution to an excessive debt problem is obvious: don't take on debt unless it is absolutely necessary, and you can afford to repay it. However, this may be easier said than done. This is especially true when you are in college, but a certain type of debt—and yes, we mean student loans—may be difficult, if not impossible, to avoid.

Student loans may need to be addressed in a separate category because there are many people who believe the ease with which students are given loans—and the large amount of loan debt they can accrue—is setting them up for financial problems later in life. From an objective standpoint, student loans do seem to defy the normal rules of smart borrowing, because they involve people who have little or no income taking on a sizable amount of debt. So you might say that student loans are their own special issue when it comes to debt. And this is something that you, and perhaps with some help from your parents, need to decide for yourself, as far as what may be a reasonable amount to borrow. To a certain extent, student loans involve a certain amount of the unknown: you are borrowing based on income you assume that you will have once you graduate. However, there are no guarantees. Many people think this is a risk worth taking because you are investing in your future professional success, and, if you do in fact become successful, this debt will more than pay for itself.

As far as other debt goes, though, you need to be very practical and only borrow as much as you can reasonably afford to repay without a lot of struggle. You do not want to end up burdening yourself with so many high monthly payments that you need to work several jobs or skip essentials like food.

FAILING TO MAKE YOUR PAYMENTS

Falling behind on your payments is one of the most common financial pitfalls. This happens very easily and for a variety of reasons. The most obvious: you simply don't have the money to make the payment. But you may also simply forget, especially if you tend to be unorganized about your due dates.

Missing even one payment can have unpleasant consequences because you will incur late fees and possibly other charges. Plus, you risk damaging your credit score.

Depending on the type of debt involved, there could also be other ramifications of a missed payment. If the payment is for an auto loan, you could risk having the car repossessed. A late rent payment could put you at risk of eviction and, at the very least, won't endear you to your landlord.

When it comes to missed payments, student loans present some of the most serious scenarios. Not only will you incur late fees and other charges, but also if your account is delinquent for a certain period of time, you will go into default. At this point, you face whopping financial penalties. Worse, the government will use its extensive resources to find ways to collect this debt from you. This could include garnishing your wages or seizing any tax refund you may be expecting. **Wage garnishment** is when your employer is required to withhold money from your pay in order to pay a debt, which could include money you owe for child support, taxes, or other obligations.

If you know that you will have trouble making a payment this month, take a proactive approach. Contact the lender or company, and explain the situation to find out what your options are. They may be able to change your due date, defer a payment, or provide other alternatives that would help you avoid late fees and any damage to your credit.

DEALING WITH DEBT COLLECTORS

One of the most dreaded of all financial scenarios is dealing with debt collectors. This is something nobody wants to experience. Unfortunately, if you don't pay your debts or fail to meet the terms of your payment agreement, you may find yourself in the uncomfortable position of dealing with debt collectors.

Debt collectors can be very persistent and aggressive when they are trying to get you to pay a debt. They will contact you frequently, possibly even on a daily basis, using a variety of methods, including mail and phone calls. And if you try to avoid them, they will often just become even more persistent.

While debt collectors may not exactly be friendly, they should behave in a professional manner. The Fair Debt Collection Practices Act is a federal set of rules that specifies what debt collectors can and cannot do while trying to collect a debt. Here are some things they cannot do:

- Call you at unreasonable hours, such as before 8 a.m. or after 9 p.m.
- Discuss your debt with anyone other than your spouse and your attorney, unless you give them permission
- Contact you at work once you've told them not to do so
- Threaten you with physical harm or use abusive or offensive language
- Misrepresent their title or position; for example, they can't claim to be an attorney or a law enforcement official
- Claim that you have committed a crime or threaten to have you arrested

If you don't think you owe the debt or think the amount due or other details are incorrect, you can dispute the debt. The collector is then required to provide verification that you do indeed owe the amount in question.

If you feel that a debt collector has broken the rules or violated your rights, you can sue them in state or federal court. However, you must file suit within a year of the violation. If you win, the debt collector may be required to pay you damages.

If you ignore the debt collector, he or she has the option of trying to sue you for the debt, although that's fairly uncommon. However, if you should receive a notice that a debt collector has initiated a legal action against you, don't ignore this! First, though, make sure it is an official legal notice. Debt collectors will sometimes send a letter that is designed to look like an official court document in order to scare you into taking action.

151

Borrowing from Undesirable Sources

Sometimes it's not just the amount you borrow that's the problem—it's where you get the money. You should avoid some sources for money at all costs. The most obvious example is anything resembling a loan shark—and yes, they do exist, and not just on television; there are many people who fall into this category. Someone may not be an official loan shark in the leg-breaking sense, but you may not want to be indebted to someone who might cause you or someone you care about serious harm.

Some people would say that parents and other relatives—as well as friends—also fall under the heading of people from whom you shouldn't borrow. This is not because you would fear physical harm but because there are emotional issues involved, especially if you have to live with the shame of not paying them back.

Another source of money that you should avoid is payday loans. These short-term loans may seem like a quick solution to an urgent money shortage, but they carry huge fees. Plus, they are designed to suck you into a continuing cycle: when payday comes, you will likely have trouble repaying this debt, so they encourage you to extend or "roll over" your balance into a new loan, which then involves even more fees. Before you know it, your balance has ballooned, and you owe much more than you realize.

Not Paying Your Taxes

Nobody enjoys paying taxes, but it's just one of those things you have to do once you become a working adult. If you have a job, you may have to pay federal income taxes. Depending on where you live, you may have to pay state and local income taxes, as well.

Your employer should be deducting taxes from your paycheck. At the end of the year, you will then file a tax return, which determines whether you still owe additional taxes, or, if you have paid too much, you will be entitled to a refund.

The good news is if you don't make a lot of money, most likely you will owe little or possibly no taxes. But this doesn't mean you can assume you don't owe anything. You should check the IRS website to see if you are required to file a return. Even if you aren't required to file, it may be to your benefit to do so because you may be eligible for some tax credits, which would entitle you to a refund. In addition, if you plan to apply for financial aid, you most likely will need to supply information from your tax return.

If you are required to file a return and fail to do so, the IRS will subject you to penalties and fines and perhaps even more serious punishment.

TIP

If you owe money for taxes but are unable to pay the full amount, you should still file your return. You can submit a form that requests a payment arrangement, which would give you more time to pay the amount you owe.

THE ONE THING YOU SHOULD NEVER, EVER DO

The worst money-related mistake you can ever make—and something you should never do, under any circumstances—is to lie on any sort of financial paperwork or application, especially anything that involves the government, such as a financial aid form, student loan application, or tax form. This can get you in serious trouble and could even result in criminal charges. You should never lie on an application, falsify records, conceal information, or otherwise engage in any sort of deceptive activity in an effort to borrow money or get any sort of financial benefit.

153

IMPORTANT THINGS TO REMEMBER

- Everyone makes an occasional mistake or bad decision when it comes to money. The important thing is that you try to minimize your mistakes and avoid common financial pitfalls as much as possible.

- Impulse buying and failure to maintain self-control when managing your money can lead to overspending and excessive debt.

- Make sure to keep track of your payment due dates, because a missed or late payment can end up costing you.

- Always tell the truth when completing any financial paperwork or application, especially anything that involves the government, such as a financial aid form, student loan application, or tax form.

CHAPTER TEN: THINKING LONG TERM

When you are young, you tend to think in terms of immediate plans: what you want to do this weekend, which classes you are taking this semester, and how you will pay your bills this month. While it's fine to think about current issues, you also should be thinking about your long-term future.

Yes, we know that things like retirement—and even marriage and kids—may seem like they are a long way off, but time has a way of passing by quickly. More important, accumulating a fund to cover these sorts of expenses can take a long time. The earlier you start, the better off you will be. Often, there are advantages to putting things in motion when you are young. With life insurance, for example, you can get a much better rate if you get a policy when you are young and healthy.

WHY START SAVING WHEN YOU ARE YOUNG?

Starting to make wise financial decisions when you are young means having more time for your investments to be in the market and potentially grow. That puts the power of compounding to work for you.

To understand how compounding works, here's a simple example from Fidelity.com that will help you see how $200 grows with a 7 percent return that compounds each year.

How compounding works...

Starting balance	Year 1 return	Ending balance	Year 2 return	Ending balance	Year 3 return	Ending balance
$200	$14 (200 x 7%)	$214	$15 (214 x 7%)	$229	$16 (229 x 7%)	$245

Over time, compounding can have a major impact on your savings. Let's say a hypothetical investor is trying to save $50,000 for retirement. That person could save $50,000 *from* income in the year of retirement, or put $5,000 away thirty-five years before retirement, assuming a 7 percent compound return. With compounding, those $5,000 annual contributions can add up.

The impact of starting early

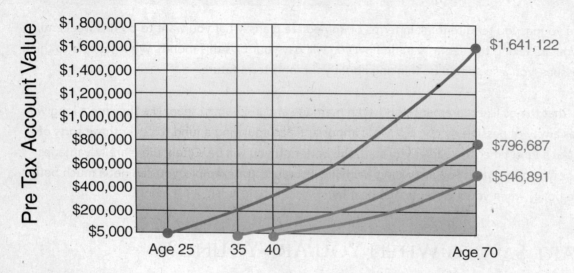

Start and end age of making annual $5,000 IRA contributions

This hypothetical example assumes the following: First, $5,000 IRA contributions on January 1st of each year for the age ranges shown; second, an annual rate of return of 7 percent; and third, no taxes on any earnings within the IRA. The ending values do not reflect taxes, fees, or inflation. If they did, the amounts would be lower. Earnings and pre-tax (deductible) contributions from Traditional IRAs are subject to taxes when withdrawn. Earnings distributed from Roth IRAs are income tax free provided certain requirements are met. IRA distributions before age 59½ may also be subject to a 10 percent penalty. (You will learn more about IRAs in the next section of this chapter.) Keep in mind that methodical investing does not ensure a profit, and it does not protect against loss in a declining market. This example is really for illustrative purposes only and does not represent the performance of any security.

The bottom line: Starting on the right path when you are young can help put you in a position to choose the kind of lifestyle and experiences you want to enjoy later on in life. In fact, with time on your side, slow and steady saving should indeed be the key to achieving your goals.

Source: https://guidance.fidelity.com/viewpoints-workplace/tips-for-young-investors-2

156

RETIREMENT PLANS

When you've just started to work, thinking about retirement may seem so far off that it's difficult to imagine. However, you don't attain a retirement fund overnight. It takes a long time to accumulate a decent-sized retirement fund, so you need to start thinking about it as early as possible. Even if you can only save a small amount, you should still get started. You may actually be surprised at how quickly even a small initial deposit can grow.

IRA PLANS

An IRA (or Individual Retirement Account) is a plan that lets you save for retirement. It's better than a regular savings account, though, because there are some tax benefits. There are a few different types of IRAs. The most common are the traditional IRA and the Roth IRA. The main difference between them relates to taxes and how they are paid. But there are other differences, too—such as restrictions on who can contribute and how much he or she can contribute—as well as rules on how you can withdraw money from your account if needed.

Don't think you have enough to put into a retirement account? According to personal finance writer, Jill Jacinto, there are a number of ways you can come up with the money. "Take a look at your daily coffee habit. Three bucks a day on the way to the office during the course of a year? Comes out to $780. Make your java at home (or buy it once a week as a treat). The sooner you do, the better off you'll be in the long run. Even if you can only contribute a few hundred bucks— you'll get the plan and pattern of saving in motion."

EXPERT ADVICE

Cristina Briboneria, CFP®, Vice President and Private Certified Financial Planner at oXYGen Financial, Inc., says it is a great idea to set up and contribute to a retirement plan while you're in school. "Students can start investing into a Roth IRA as long as they have earned income. The maximum you can put into a Roth IRA is $5,500 for 2013. Why a Roth? Well, the money that you contribute is after-tax, grows tax-free, and then you can withdraw it tax-free for the four following reasons:

1. First-time home purchase
2. School tuition
3. Medical expenses
4. Retirement

Typically people who are still in school have very low income tax; therefore, they get to take advantage of this benefit of not paying much tax on their contribution and not having to pay tax in the future.

Assume the following: Save $50 for four years. A rate of return of 6 percent per year by the time you are out of school will not be $2,400 ($50 times 48 months); it will be $2,704.89 after four years. This difference can be considered significant especially if you're just getting out of school, and you are trying to raise money for the down payment of your first home."

401(K)

A 401(k) is another type of retirement plan, but this one is usually set up through your employer. It lets you save a portion of your income before the deduction of taxes, so just as with an IRA, there are some tax benefits to this plan.

The money you put into a 401(k) is invested, usually into a variety of sources—usually a combination of stocks, bonds, and other types of investments. In addition to the money you contribute, your employer contributes to your fund. However, an employer usually doesn't start contributing until after you've worked for the company for a certain period of time.

One of the downsides of a 401(k) is that it can be difficult, and in some cases almost impossible, to access the money in your account if you want to use it before you are eligible for retirement. If you can make a withdrawal (and the rules related to withdrawals vary by plan), you will be subject to hefty taxes and possibly other penalties.

"In 2008, we saw way too many people making short-term decisions about their 401(k)'s by moving the money into a safer investment like money market accounts," notes Patrick Patterson, who worked at that time as a financial services manager at Freedom One Financial Group. "They did this to keep their money in a safer place when the market took a hefty downturn. However, when the market trended upwards, their money did not go back up or grow like it could have. As result, they may have less money in their account than what they put in." Patterson adds that "had the decision been made based on the long term, and they kept their money invested in the market, the result would have been a higher account balance than ever before, and they would have made a lot of money as the market continued to rebound." Patterson concludes, "In the history of the market, there has never been one time the market did not recover. Stay in for the long term, and you'll be fine."

BORROWING FROM YOUR 401(K)

Some 401(k) plans allow you to borrow from your account. This really is not a loan because you aren't requesting credit or money from a lender. Basically, you are accessing your own money from your retirement plan, but it is viewed as a loan because these funds must be repaid according to specific terms.

According to Rich Rausser, Senior Vice President of Client Services at Pentegra Retirement Services, you should give this a lot of thought before taking this type of loan. "Although many 401(k) plans allow you to borrow money from your account for up to five years, and the interest you pay back over those five years through payroll deductions is going back into your 401(k), that money is, by definition, meant for your retirement. And with the money you are borrowing being withdrawn from your plan, you will miss any gains in those funds while your money is being spent elsewhere."

Rausser adds, "Similarly, if you leave your job, companies will often issue you a check covering your 401(k) balance. This can be a significant amount and viewed as a "windfall of free money" by those who may feel tempted to splurge on something they otherwise could not afford. The fact is, you probably can't afford it— at least where your retirement is concerned. Instead, deposit those funds into a rollover IRA or similar account within 60 days (to avoid taxes and penalties). If you left your job to take another one, roll your old

401(k) into one that your new company offers. Maintaining separate accounts under different employers does not make sense, and it is hardly the kind of thing you want to be spending your time sorting out when you reach retirement age."

EXPERT ADVICE

Scott Laue, financial advisor with Savant Capital Management, shares these basic steps for young people to start thinking about their long-term future:

- **The first step is participating in your company 401(k) plan.** Taking advantage of this employee benefit can mean more money in your pocket later and a more satisfying retirement. Contributing money to a 401(k) gives you an immediate tax deduction, which means lower taxable income, convenient payroll deductions, and possibly a matching contribution from your employer.

- **If your employer does offer a company match, take full advantage of it.** Employer matches are one of the most powerful forces in retirement saving, and if you don't utilize it, you're essentially throwing away free money. Typically, an employer match is a percentage of what you contribute to the plan up to a maximum amount—for example, 50 cents of every dollar up to 6 percent of your salary; this would mean a 3 percent employer contribution to you if you contribute 6 percent of your pay.

- **Be proactive and start saving early.** Map out a savings plan that works for you, and then determine approximately how much money you'll need to save each year between now and your retirement. If possible, save more than you think you'll need to provide an extra cushion. Setting aside more money now helps to build a larger nest egg for your retirement. Plus, don't forget to increase your contribution amount when your salary increases.

- **Maintain a well-diversified portfolio.** Your portfolio should contain stocks of different sizes, bonds, money market funds, and other asset classes. The market has been a roller coaster over the last few years, and remaining diverse in your investments will help you preserve the principal while maximizing returns and minimizing risks.

160

LIFE INSURANCE

For many young people, life insurance is something they rarely think about. They assume they don't need to worry about this for a long time and that this is something they should look into once they are older.

However, the opposite is true. The best time to get life insurance is when you are young. Insurance companies base rates on several factors, all of which they use to determine your level of risk. As a young person, the insurance company considers you a low risk, meaning, you are unlikely to die or become disabled, so your rates will be very low. By getting the policy when you are young, you can take advantage of these low rates. By contrast, if you wait, the cost will go up. The older you are, the more expensive it will be to get life insurance coverage.

INVESTMENTS

One of the main ways that you can prepare for your long-term financial needs is through investments. These can involve a variety of different types of financial instruments, including stocks, bonds, and money market accounts.

One important aspect of investing is the element of risk. There is always the possibility that you won't make any profit, or that you could lose some or all of the money you invested. The risk varies depending on the type of investment. Some investments, like bonds, carry little or no risk. The downside is that you won't earn as much profit from this low-risk choice. In order to possibly earn large profits, you will need to take some risks.

WHAT DO MILLENNIALS KNOW ABOUT INVESTING?

Here are some interesting stats from the Spectrem Group, a consulting and research firm specializing in wealth management and retirement markets:

- Millennials (those born after 1980) are significantly more likely to use social media channels, such as Facebook, LinkedIn, and Twitter, when making their financial decisions than their slightly older counterparts, the Gen X (those born between 1965 and 1980) investors.

161

- Millennial investors are the most optimistic about their future, with approximately 70 percent believing their personal financial situation will be stronger one year from now. Despite their optimism, they are still quite conservative, with less than half willing to take any significant risk on a portion of their investments in order to earn a high rate of return.

- When it comes to factors that influence an investor's investment selection, millennial generation investors are more concerned with the social responsibility of the investments than any other generation and significantly more than the World War II generation. This, in part, has to do with millennial investors growing up in a time when social responsibility, in general, is instilled in them from early on in their lives.

STOCK MARKET

One of the most popular ways to invest is through the stock market. A stock is a piece of ownership in a company. So, yes, you could technically say you are a part owner of a company, but your piece of the company is usually very, very small. When you buy stock in a company, you are a shareholder in that company.

Stock traders buy and sell stocks on the stock market. The goal is to buy a stock at a cheap price and then sell it once it is worth a lot more. This is buying low and selling high.

The stock market can involve a lot of risk, and it is not for the faint-hearted; it can be like a roller coaster. Within a span of a week, your stock's value may go up and down and up and down again. No one guarantees a stock's value. There is the possibility that you could lose most or all of your money. You could also make a huge profit.

Not all companies have stock available. A company sells shares in order to raise money to expand or hire more employees or for other reasons.

DIVIDENDS

Dividends are profits you get from your investment as a shareholder of a company. Reinvesting those dividends is a popular and effective way to help your money grow.

Marc Lichtenfeld, Associate Investment Director of The Oxford Club and author of *Get Rich with Dividends*, says, "The secret is to invest in quality stocks that raise the dividend every year and reinvest those dividends to take advantage of compounding. Using this method, and picking the right stocks, there is no reason why someone shouldn't be able to generate a return of 12 percent per year over the long term. That kind of return triples your money over ten years and grows it by 10 times over twenty years. It's easy, very inexpensive, and has been proven to work over decades of market ups and downs."

He continues, "It's very simple. Once you find a stock (or stocks), you buy it (them) and instruct your broker to reinvest the dividends. Let's say you bought 50 shares of a $20 stock for $1,000. And let's say the stock pays a dividend of $1 per share every year. If you reinvest the dividend, it means you automatically buy more shares with the dividend rather than taking the cash. That first year you will earn $50 in cash, which is used to buy 2.5 more shares. The next year, you will earn dividends on 52.5 shares, not 50, and you will earn $52.50, which is used to buy more shares, which spin off more dividends, which buy more shares, etc. Compounding works its magic over time, and the amount of income that is generated becomes substantial in relation to your original investment. In year 10, you're earning nearly 20 percent per year on your original investment. By year 20, you're earning just about 100 percent per year on your investment."

Lichtenfeld notes that you can stop reinvesting at any time and simply collect the dividend in cash if you need it. "Plus," he adds, "if you do this strategy in a retirement account, the dividends are tax deferred until you retire decades from now. Furthermore, this strategy works even when the market is bad. In fact, for a young investor, the strategy works better when the market is bad because when the stock goes down, you can buy more shares."

Going back to the original example where you bought 2.5 shares of stock at $20 with the $50 dividend, Lichtenfeld says, "If the stock price has declined to $15, you can now buy 3.3 shares. Keep in mind that the dividend does not decrease just because the stock price did. So now, you own 53.3 shares instead of 52.5. Now, you'll earn $53.30 in dividends instead of $52.50, which is used to purchase more stock, etc."

EXPERT ADVICE

Chris Sands, Vice President and Private CFO® Specialist at oXYGen Financial, Inc., shares these quick tips to help you save or invest your money:

- **Track your money!** It is so important to just know where your dollars are going, both from a savings and expenses standpoint, as well as a rate of return standpoint. We give our clients their own online Financial Dashboard where they can link all of their bank accounts and credit cards to track their spending, show them trends, and review spending vs. savings habits. On a less-detailed scale, people can use the free services of Mint.com (http://www.mint.com/) to do this. Software to track these things is great, but you actually have to use it actively.

- **Rate of Savings will ALWAYS, ALWAYS, ALWAYS beat Rate of Return, period!** The point is that you systematically pay yourself first. My next couple of tips will detail how. But this takes the pressure off of having to get a great Rate of Return. A lot of people fall into the trap of believing that if they can get a great rate of return somewhere, they won't have to save as much. It's actually the reverse. When you are young and just getting started, first you have to build this foundation of good savings habits. Save three months' worth of living expenses to "Emergency Cash Reserves", contribute some to a 401(k) or other retirement plan, and start an investment/brokerage account and add small amounts to it regularly.

- **Save 20%!** It is statistically proven that one major differentiating factor between those who are successful in their retirement vs. those who are not is that successful people saved at least 20 percent of their Gross Income. This number is trending closer to a required 25 percent savings as pensions are becoming extinct, and Social Security is on the endangered species list. As a Millennial, I don't think I will see any of it, do you?! So it makes it that much more important for Millennials to save over 20 percent, as opposed to their Baby Boomer parents and grandparents who might have gotten away with saving 10 percent because they got Social Security benefits or were lucky enough to have a pension.

164

WHERE TO PUT YOUR SAVINGS

So where should you put your savings? There's no one right answer to that question. The best choice for you will depend on a variety of factors, including your age, income, employment situation, and long-term goals.

If you just want to stash your money in a safe place, a plain old savings account or CD will do fine. However, your money will grow very slowly because the interest rate on these types of accounts is relatively low.

If you do have the option of contributing to a 401(k) or IRA, you definitely should consider it because it gives you the opportunity to take advantage of tax benefits and enjoy a better rate of growth than putting it in a money market fund or CD.

And if you aren't afraid of some risk, consider investments. Again, the level of risk involved depends on the types of investments you choose.

IMPORTANT THINGS TO REMEMBER

- Now is the time to start thinking about your long-term financial plans. Putting accounts and other systems in place now will help you get a head start and give your money a chance to grow for a longer period of time.

- Retirement plans such as an IRA or 401(k) are great ways to save your money while also enjoying tax benefits.

- It is much easier, and less expensive, to obtain life insurance now than it will be when you are older.

MONEY QUIZ

DO YOUR MONEY SMARTS MAKE THE GRADE?

Take this little quiz to determine if your "money smarts" make the grade.

True or False: Read each statement and determine whether it is true or false.

True	False	
__True	__False	**1.** You want to purchase a $40 shirt at the mall. Your summer job pays $8 an hour. You will only need to work 5 hours to earn the $40 needed for the shirt.
__True	__False	**2.** There's no need to match the checks you've written and debit card purchases you've made to your bank statement, because you can check your account balance over the phone or online anytime you need to know it.
__True	__False	**3.** After pulling an all-nighter studying for an exam, you need a cappuccino to keep you awake for the test. Your bank's website shows that you have $25 left in your account. As you head to the coffee shop to purchase your cappuccino, you would be safe in assuming the debit card won't be declined because there are certainly sufficient funds.
__True	__False	**4.** The close quarters of most college dormitories means college students are at a high risk for identity theft.
__True	__False	**5.** As long as you still have money at the end of the week, you don't really need to keep track of where you're spending your money.
__True	__False	**6.** Maggie has $1,000 worth of credit card debt and tries to pay the minimum balance each month. Sometimes she pays a few days late or forgets to pay at all. But she knows that won't affect her credit score because she's just a college student.

__True	__False	**7.** Marcus receives a $200 monthly allowance from his parents to help cover his school expenses. He also has a part-time job and earns about $300 a month (after taxes). Marcus must spend $150 on rent and $100 on car insurance. If he budgets $85 for eating out, $45 for clothes, and $50 for everything else, it will take him eight months to accumulate savings of $500.
__True	__False	**8.** A thief steals your credit card and racks up $2,000 worth of charges. You notify your credit card company as soon as you realize the card is missing, but you must pay off the $2,000 bill charged by the thieves.
__True	__False	**9.** Sales taxes are not deducted from your paycheck by the federal government.
__True	__False	**10.** Using a cross-cut shredder to destroy credit card applications and sensitive personal information like Social Security numbers is an effective way to prevent identity theft.

DO YOUR MONEY SMARTS MAKE THE GRADE?

ANSWERS:

1. False. While it is true that working 5 hours at $8 per hour will earn a gross pay of $40, your take-home pay will be less than that. Federal income tax, Social Security, and Medicare contributions are withheld from your check, and that means you'll need to work a few extra hours to buy that new shirt.

2. False. Comparing your check register to the bank statement can be time-consuming. However, it's the only way to know that your records match the bank's records. Banks do make errors from time to time, and you generally only have 60 days to notify the bank about their mistake.

3. False. While it is true that most debit cards won't work if you don't have enough money in your checking account to cover a specific charge, that won't always save you from having your bank charge you a fee (often $35 or more) for having insufficient funds. For example, you forgot that you wrote a $22 check at the mall the day before the big exam. That check hasn't cleared yet, but you'll only have $3 left in your account once it does—not enough to cover that cappuccino and making it a very expensive energy booster.

4. True. College students are prime targets for identity theft. Dorm rooms and apartments are often shared, giving many people easy access to personal information. Keep track of credit card receipts and statements, as well as checkbooks, personal identification numbers (PINs), and other banking information. Also, safeguard your Social Security number. Choose alternate numbers for campus identification and grade posting.

5. False. Even if you still have money left over at the end of the week, it's a good idea to keep track of where your money is going. The trick is to know how much money you have, what you need to buy, and when you need to buy it. Are you spending $50 a week on pizza? You might be able to afford it now, but what happens when your car breaks down? Create a monthly spending plan with broad categories (rent, tuition, eating out, movies, and so on) that will be easy for you to monitor.

6. False. Maggie is hurting her credit score each time she pays her bill late or doesn't pay it at all. While it's true that she might not purchase a home until she's older, credit scores come into play for apartment rentals, loan interest rates, and even on job searches. These days, many employers check credit scores of potential new employees during the hiring process. To maintain a good credit rating, pay your bills on time and don't overextend yourself credit-wise.

7. True. If Marcus sticks with his spending plan, he should be able to save about $70 each month. In eight months, he'll have about $560 set aside in savings.

8. False. As long as you report the stolen credit card to your card issuer, your maximum liability under federal law for unauthorized use of your credit card is $50 per card. The thieves may have illegally charged $2,000 on your card, but your credit card issuer can't hold you accountable for any unauthorized charges beyond the $50 limit.

9. True. Sales taxes are added to the purchase of certain goods and services, not withheld from your paycheck.

10. True. For extra protection, consider purchasing a cross-cut shredder to destroy all credit card applications and other sensitive personal information.

SCORES:

If you correctly answered eight or more of these questions, you've clearly paid attention in reading this book and are ready to **move to the head of the money smarts class**.

Did you give the right answers to six or more of these questions? You might need to r**eview your money skills** and get a better grip on your finances.

If you correctly answered five or fewer of these financial questions, then **Money Management 101 might be a good option** for you. As you've seen throughout the guide, it's important to become proficient in personal finance matters. You might not really need a formal college course, but by reading, attending community workshops, and seeking professional advice, you can access the information you need to make the most of your money—now and in the future.

Source: http://valueyourmoney.org/quiz/moneysmarts_q.asp

GLOSSARY

Adjustable rate: an interest rate that can change depending on the economy or other circumstances

Annual fee: fee a credit card company will charge you just for having the card, whether you use it or not. Not all cards have an annual fee; for those that do, the fee can vary widely.

Annual Percentage Rate (APR): yearly interest rate you will be charged for any balance you carry on a credit card

Asset: something that will rise in price and can be sold for more money

ATM: Automated Teller Machine, which you can use to make deposits and withdraw cash from your bank account

Balance: amount of money in your bank account at a given time; amount owed on a credit card

Bond: sold to get money to start up a business or support the government. It collects some interest over time.

Borrow: to take out a loan. You obtain money from a person or business (usually a bank or loan agency) and agree to pay it back with interest.

Bounced check: a check that exceeds the balance of your bank account and causes your account to become overdrawn (go into the negative). Your bank may honor the check or return it unpaid, but, either way, they will probably charge you a fee.

Budget: a plan of how you will spend and/or save your money

Capital: money used to start up a business or fund a project

Compound interest: when interest accumulates and is added to the principal, causing a sort of "snowball effect." You end up paying or earning interest on previous interest charges that have been added to the principal.

Contract: a written agreement between two people or parties that spells out the terms for a loan, sale, or other business transaction

Co-signer: someone who signs a loan or rental application with you. This person agrees to be responsible for that debt, should you fail to pay it.

Credit report: a history of what you have borrowed and how you have paid your debts

Credit score: a 3-digit number that is calculated based on your credit report. Lenders and businesses use your credit score to decide whether to approve you for credit or a loan.

Debit Card: card linked to a bank account, usually a checking account, used to pay for things instead of cash or check. You can only spend as much as you have in your bank account at that time; otherwise, your transaction will probably be declined, or your account will become overdrawn.

Debt: money that you owe to someone. Debt is often the result of a loan or a credit account.

Deposit: money put into a bank account

Direct deposit: when your paycheck or other payment is automatically deposited into your bank account

EFC: Expected Family Contribution, a figure calculated by the government to help determine your financial need for student aid. The higher your EFC, the less chance you have of receiving financial aid.

FDIC: Federal Deposit Insurance Corporation, a federal agency that insures your bank account, covering your deposits (up to $250,000)

FICA: Federal Insurance Contributions Act, which allows for deduction from your paycheck to fund Social Security and Medicare programs

Finance charge: costs that a business (such as a bank or credit company) adds to your debt as a fee for providing or servicing the loan or account

Fixed rate: an interest rate that stays at one amount for the length of the loan

Grace period: period of time during which you can pay your balance without any interest charges

Gross pay: amount you earn before deductions

Income: money that you earn as pay for doing a job

Inflation: a rise in the prices for goods and services over time

Installment loan: a type of credit in which you borrow a certain amount of money that is to be used for a specific purpose. You must make a monthly payment until the balance is paid off. Examples of installment loans are mortgages and car payments.

Interest: fee paid to use money. When you deposit money in an account, you earn interest. When you borrow money, you pay interest.

Introductory rate: a low interest rate a credit card company offers you for a short time when you first open an account

Line of credit: a preapproved loan that you can get money from as you need it. You only borrow what you need (or want) and only pay interest on that amount.

Medicare: an insurance program that is run by the federal government and provides medical insurance to the elderly and disabled. The program is funded through taxes that are collected in the form of payroll deductions.

Minimum payment: the lowest amount you can pay on your monthly bill for a credit card account to keep the account in good status. If you only pay the minimum every month, you will end up paying a lot of interest charges.

Mortgage: loan from the bank used to buy a house

Net pay: amount of your actual paycheck after all deductions. This can often be shocking, because the deductions can often take a big chunk of your paycheck.

PIN: Personal Identification Number, the security code used to access your account

Prime rate: the lowest rate of interest at which money may be borrowed commercially; an interest rate formally announced by a bank to be the lowest available at a particular time to its most credit-worthy customers (also referred to as prime interest rate)

Principal: the amount of money you borrow (or deposited into an account) before any interest charges are added

Profit: money you make when you sell something, after deducting all of your expenses and costs

Resume: a document that lists your work experience, education, references, and other important information that potential employers (or customers) would want to know. You use this when you are trying to get a job.

Revolving credit: a type of credit account that you can keep using over and over, assuming you make your required payments and stay under your credit limit. Also known as a revolving account, it includes credit cards and home equity lines of credit.

Routing number: the first set of numbers at the bottom left side of your check

Rule of 72: a handy little trick to estimate how long it will take for your money to double in an interest-earning account. You divide 72 by the interest rate, and that tells you how long it will take to double your money.

Secured credit card: a credit account for which you deposit a certain amount to guarantee the debt. You can only borrow an equivalent to your deposit amount, and if you don't pay your bill, your deposit is used to satisfy the debt.

Social engineering: the process of manipulating or tricking you into doing a certain action or revealing information

---

174

Social Security: a federal government program that provides monetary benefits for the elderly, disabled, and (in some cases) survivors of individuals who have died; these payments are funded by money collected in the form of deductions from paychecks.

Stock: partial ownership of a company

Stock market: the system for buying and selling shares for different companies

Variable rate: percentage rate that may change over time, based on the current prime lending rate or according to the terms spelled out in your contract with the lender

Withdrawal: money taken out of an account

RESOURCES

WEB SITES

Annual Credit Report

https://www.annualcreditreport.com

Official site where you can request your free credit reports.

Better Money Habits

BetterMoneyHabits.com

Created by Bank of America and Khan Academy to provide free, self-paced, easy-to-understand resources to develop better money habits, the site features educational videos that take a bite-sized, plain-language approach to simplifying complex topics such as setting and sticking to a budget, ways to save, understanding how interest works, and more.

Budget Diet

www.thebudgetdiet.com/

Tips for finding deals and saving money.

CareerBuilder

www.careerbuilder.com/

Job search site.

Credit Karma

https://www.creditkarma.com/

Free credit scores and credit monitoring.

CSS/Financial Aid PROFILE®

http://student.collegeboard.org/css-financial-aid-profile

Online form used by many private colleges for non-federal financial aid.

eBay

www.ebay.com/

Make money by selling your items on this auction site.

eHealthInsurance

http://www.ehealthinsurance.com/

Health insurance shopping and comparison site.

Equifax

www.equifax.com

Phone: 800-685-1111 (toll-free)

One of the three major credit bureaus.

Etsy

www.etsy.com/

Earn extra cash by selling crafts and other homemade items.

Experian

www.experian.com

Phone: 888-397-3742 (toll-free)

One of the three major credit bureaus.

FAFSA

www.fafsa.ed.gov

Free Application for Federal Student Aid, which is required for any federal student aid.

FatWallet

www.fatwallet.com/

Find out about hot deals, coupon codes, and "inside secrets" from bargain hunters.

FinAid

www.finaid.org/

Comprehensive source of information and advice related to financial aid. The site also has links to a bunch of scholarship search sites.

FTC Identity Theft Site

www.ftc.gov/idtheft

Get tips on protecting yourself from identity theft and what to do if you believe you've been a victim of identity theft.

Garage Sale Gal

www.garagesalegal.com/

Tips and advice on finding great deals at garage sales—or hosting an awesome garage sale of your own.

H&R Block Dollars and Sense

www.hrblockdollarsandsense.com/

Offering personal finance education for teens, this site also has a scholarship challenge where groups of teens from across the country can compete for several scholarships.

Indeed

www.indeed.com/

Job listing search tool.

Internal Revenue Service (IRS)

www.irs.gov/

The agency in charge of collecting federal taxes. On its site, you can find out all about the tax forms you may need to complete, tax deductions, and how to fill out a tax return.

Mint.com

https://www.mint.com/

Find lots of cool money management and budgeting resources here, including tools that let you create colorful charts and graphs showing where your money goes.

Money Crashers

www.MoneyCrashers.com

Advice and information related to money and careers, with a special focus on issues of interest to young people.

My First Financial Planner

www.myfirstfinancialplanner.com/

Low-cost financial planning services for young people.

National Student Loan Data System

www.nslds.ed.gov/nslds_SA/

The U.S. Department of Education's (ED's) central database for student aid, NSLDS receives data from schools, guaranty agencies, the Direct Loan program, and other Department of Education programs. NSLDS Student Access provides a centralized, integrated view of Title IV loans and grants so that recipients of Title IV aid can access and inquire about their Title IV loans and/or grant data.

PayCheckCity

www.paycheckcity.com/

Paycheck tools and calculators.

PayDivvy

www.paydivvy.com

This website, which allows you to pay a variety of bills online from one place, also has a cool feature that helps you gather payment for those bills you are splitting with other people.

Pinecone Research

www.pineconeresearch.com/

Get paid to take surveys or try out products

Practical Money Skills for Life

www.practicalmoneyskills.com/

Financial literacy tools, games, and information for teens, adults, and educators.

PROFILE®

See: CSS/Financial Aid PROFILE®.

SavingForCollege

www.savingforcollege.com

Lots of information on financial aid and ways to save and pay for college.

Scholarship America

www.scholarshipamerica.org

Scholarship and education support organization.

SimplyHired

www.simplyhired.com/

Job search site.

TheMint.org

http://themint.org/

Sponsored by The Northwestern Mutual Foundation, this website offers lots of information and helpful tools on money-related topics.

TransUnion

www.transunion.com

Phone: 877-322-8228 (toll-free for a free credit report)

One of the three major credit bureaus.

Your Smart Money Moves

www.yoursmartmoneymoves.com

Financial blog for the X and Y Generations.